My Purpose Is For Real:

7 SIMPLE STEPS TO GET BACK ON TRACK TO ACHIEVE YOUR DREAMS

Tiffany D. Sanders, Ph.D.

Author's Disclaimer:

The instructions, suggestions, recommendations and advice in this book are not intended as a substitute for psychological counseling or clinical advice from a licensed professional. Please consult a qualified mental health counselor or medical professional for clinical advice or psychological counseling. This book absolves itself from responsibility or liability for any actions or inactions taken by the reader based on claims advocated or discussed in the book. In the interest of confidentiality and preserving the privacy and rights of the individuals presented in this book, names, and in some cases, identifying information have been changed. However, the results from the recommendations, persona stories, scenarios, circumstances, and situations are real.

A Diverse Legacy, Incorporated Book
Published by Diverse Legacy
Copyright © 2011 Diverse Legacy, Corporation
All rights reserved. No part of this book can be reproduced or distributed in any form by any means, without the expressed written prior consent of the author and publisher.

ISBN: 0984679790
ISBN-13: 9780984679799

Manufactured in the United States of America

Dedication

This book is dedicated to:
My Parents, Lon and Yvonne Sanders,
My Brother, Shon Brown, and
My Sisters, Shinese Brown, LaKeisha Sanders, and Tonya Sanders,
My Lovely Nieces, Breanna, Keeara, and Kennedy, and
My Friends and Loved Ones who have and continue
to support everything I do in life.
A special thanks to my best friends, Melanie Williams
and Ericka Burnett, and my editor, James McCallum. I love you.

Table of Contents

Purpose Assessment Quiz

Please answer the following questions. If you answer yes to 5 or more questions, then this book is for you!

1. Are you working a job where you are unhappy?

2. Are you tired of living paycheck to paycheck?

3. Do you wish you were doing something more fulfilling and exciting in your life?

4. Are their past disappointments in your life that paralyze you from moving forward in life?

5. Do you fear making a change in your life or career?

6. Do you want to set a better example for your children about the importance of living a purpose filled life?

7. Do you think it is too late to live a purpose filled life?

8. Do you desire to get your life in order and minimize distractions so you can focus on achieving your dreams?

9. Do you engage in negativistic thinking that make you feel unworthy of living a life full of joy and passion?

10. Are you ready to make the necessary sacrifices to see your dreams come to life?

Foreword

Dr. Tiffany D. Sanders is a young lady on the cutting edge in the fields of Psychology and Family and Child Studies. Tiffany, as she is more affectionately known, is the success of Chicago. Tiffany completed her doctoral studies in School Psychology at the University of Florida, became a licensed psychologist, opened her own business, and has published this, her first book, all before she reached the age of 32. What an adventure this was for Tiffany! She proved to the world that all things are possible to those who believe in God.

The reason I call Tiffany Chicago's success is because her life was headed in a much different path before a major intervention by God. Tiffany had all of the smarts to do anything she would put her mind to, but she lacked the focus and determination to order things correctly. Tiffany was able to see the victory after her fall from grace when she encountered perhaps the worst thing that could happen to a person. She was threatened with being expelled from college and losing everything that had been invested in her by those who loved her. This major crisis enabled the real woman to see what she had not seen before, dreams, aspirations, and a future filled with happiness. All of this was threatened to be cut off, but thank God He looked beyond all that she had gone through and encouraged her to rise.

In rising to where she is today, Tiffany knows who holds her future and the outlook is positive. Tiffany can now take her place among the pioneers who dared to be different and make a profound impact in the lives of people. The secret is out, and the wisdom, knowledge and understanding on how to get back on track and stake your claim to a brighter tomorrow will be revealed in this new book!! Step out on faith and allow the stories in this book to inspire and guide you.

Tiffany climbed the ladder that reaches upward not for herself but for those she desires to see helped.

I have personally watched and followed Tiffany and have been inspired to achieve my dreams too. This book will speak to a man or woman, the young and the old, the loss and found. I am a firm believer that we should never stop growing, and Tiffany has found a way to make this dream possible.

Introduction

Some who are reading this book may be upset that are reading a book about "purpose." From elementary school through high school, they were extremely bright. They came from a family of accomplished people; people who instinctively knew their purpose in life. They *know* they possess talent and intelligence capable of building their own success. However, for the life of them, it escapes them as to why they do not know the steps to discover their purpose.

Let me assure you, people of many stripes go through life unsure of their purpose. They enjoy their current job, but believe they should be doing more in life, and for whatever reason they are lost as to the process of getting further in life? Keep reading this book. It is designed especially for you. I will give you simple steps to take to get your life back on track.

This book is also designed for individuals who were on track and got derailed. This is just as frustrating as not knowing your purpose. Why? Because either way, you are not living up to your

God given potential, nor are you enjoying the life He wants you to have. So let's get started.

What Knocked You Off Course?

Think back to when you were in middle school when your homeroom teacher asked, "What would you like to be when you grow up?" Bright eyed and bushy tailed, you responded, "I want to be a CEO, doctor, lawyer, fireman, police officer or an astronaut!!" However, as you became older, cultivated hobbies and interests, and were exposed to more professions, your desires and interests changed. You no longer wanted to be those things. Yet, you still wanted to have a successful career that would allow you to have a positive impact on your community and the lives of those close to you. So you began to plan things out.

In high school you began studying harder to bring your grades up. You stayed after school to get extra help from the teacher. You took a prep course to improve your ACT or SAT scores and joined a couple of clubs to enhance your college application. You even cut out skateboarding or playing a game of basketball with the fellas every night, slanging dope, gang banging or just macking with the girls after school because you were determined to bring your GPA up. You believed in yourself, and it worked!!! You were accepted into college. You majored in Accounting, English, or Biology and were well on your way to being a college graduate. Yippee!!

But what happened? The Bible says in Hebrews 12: 1-2 *Let us run with perseverance the race marked out for us.* What got in your way of reaching your goals? You were running such a good race. You were running the last curve and kicked it into high gear, but you never crossed the finish line. Who or what knocked you off track? Or did you get in your own way? How did your four year college plan turn into a lifetime goal?

❖ Reflect upon and list the obstacles in your path that nearly knocked you off course.

MY STORY

Did you get knocked off track just as you began to lay the foundation for creating the life that you wanted to live? I, too, was like you in high school. I buckled down and concentrated on my work the last couple of years of school to ensure my acceptance into a good university. As I researched different schools that offered my major in physical therapy, I began to map out my future. In the process of buckling down, I performed well enough to increase my GPA, was inducted into the National Honor Society and accepted at the college of my choice.

What happened? How did I *almost* get in the way of what was predestined for me?

Although I diligently worked to improve my grades and performance in school, I did not put the same amount of effort into addressing my emotional well-being and anger issues. Many of my clients and friends always find this hard to believe, but I used to have serious anger management issues. Yes, me!!

Throughout my life, I was quick tempered, easily irritated, and flippant. I frequently found myself getting into arguments and fights with the children in my neighborhood and at school. By no means was I a tough guy or the queen bee, but my lack of emotional regulation or fiery temper caused me to be suspended in junior high, high school, and worse – college! By the time I graduated high school, I had been in five fights at school (more at home with my family members and in the neighborhood), which resulted in numerous suspensions. I once got suspended for fighting a friend the Friday before finals began.

Clearly, I was not making smart decisions, and failed to realize that I was undermining myself from reaching my goal of having a successful life. I quickly wised up that I was spending too much time getting into fights over silly issues, and fighting wasn't lady like or cute. At that time, I was in a relationship with my high school sweetheart and I did not like the image I was presenting to him. I quickly cut out the fighting, but I never addressed the anger issues.

A tough summer that included a break-up with my high school sweetheart left me drained, emotionally hurt, and angry. I was left feeling drained, emotionally hurt, and angry. Shortly after I started my freshman year of college, I had another altercation with a girl who lived in my dorm. The first verbal altercation did not lead to a physical fight, but the second one did. We were both reprimanded by the Office of Judicial Affairs. However, I ended up with a more severe punishment since I punched the other girl, who was three months pregnant. I was back to making bad decisions. I was arrested, charged with battery, and expelled from college. This was the absolute lowest moment of my life. I was disappointed with myself and the direction that I was headed. My parents had to get me a lawyer in order to fight the legal charges, and I had to overcome my feelings of failure and disappointment.

Undoubtedly because of God's unmerited favor and his loving arms of forgiveness, my expulsion was commuted and I was given probation for a year. As long as I stayed out of trouble, I could remain in college. Further grace was extended by God when the charges were eventually dropped and the case was dismissed. However, the stress of dealing with Judicial Affairs, battling a court case, and subsequently getting kicked out of college took its toll on me and my grades. I did not earn the GPA I needed to get accepted into the Physical Therapy program. Unfortunately, the race that I had been running was quickly coming to an end. I knocked myself off course.

WHAT IS YOUR STORY?

Maybe your story involved the death of a loved one in an unexpected or tragic manner. This loved one was your rock. He or she buffered you from anguish and helped you remain strong, especially when times were rough. Their untimely death left you feeling empty, unmotivated, and pondering which way to go. Instead of finishing your degree, you opted to quit school and got a job making $7 to $10 dollars an hour. Although that job allowed you to make ends meet, you were left feeling unfulfilled deep inside. No amount of money in the world can eliminate your desire to have purpose in your life. So at the start of the New Year, you made a resolution to go back to school to finish your degree. The busyness of life (e.g., children, marriage, work, or other responsibilities) has prevented you from seeing that goal to completion.

Perhaps that is not your story. Maybe you had a baby during your high school or college years. As a result, you had to get a job to pay for diapers, day care, doctors' visits, clothes, food, and birthday parties. Your plans and priorities changed. You jumped from job to job, looking for something better or more stable. Now you decide to pursue a career as a hair stylist or nail technician. You make good money, but the long hours of being away from your child and not working in a field that you loved, leave you feeling frustrated and wanting something more out of life.

Or did you get caught up in the wrong crowd when you were in junior high or high school? Instead of spending time after school studying, doing your school work, helping out around the house, or after school practicing your jump shot, you were on the corner slanging, selling, chiefing or hanging with the fellas. You thought it was more important to be loyal to your boys and get into fights with others who were challenging your territory, or to sell drugs to earn quick money. You thought your focus was to floss, wear the nicest clothes, chase skirts, get rims on your car, stay out late, party or get into mischief. As a teenager you thought this was the life for you and you wanted nothing more. When your parents were suggesting otherwise, you did not listen. They sounded like a broken record. Little did you know the behavior you demonstrated was knocking you off track, undermining your future and affecting your life. Now you are in your late 20s, 30s, 40s, and 50s saying "I wish I would have done better in school and with my life. I wish I did not waste my time, energy and resources doing stupid stuff. I should be better off in life. I should own my house, have my own business, drive a better car and have more money saved."

So you decided to pursue a career in real estate. You go to school to become a realtor, you study hard, and sit for the exam. You take the state exam and unfortunately you failed it. You are discouraged, upset, and angry at yourself. Your confidence drops. You are frustrated, and you feel like a failure. Do not fret, my dear friend because this book is for you, too. By the end of this book, you will learn strategies that will get you back on track to discover your purpose, to achieve your dreams, and to take care of your family.

ARE YOU STUCK IN A RUT?

You currently have a secure job working for a company with great benefits, vacation time, good hours and good pay. Perhaps you have a loving husband, two beautiful children and a charming house. You are living the good life – or just maybe a little beyond your means and you come to grips with this gnawing feeling in your stomach - you feel unfulfilled and believe that your life is boring. Your children are growing up and they do not need you as much any longer. You have helped support your husband or wife in their career while neglecting the fact that you have none. You constantly criticize yourself for choosing the "safe route" in life and debate your purpose outside of being a wife and a mother or a husband and a father. Realizing that there is more to life than bringing home a paycheck every two weeks, or being a stay at home mother or father, or a supportive spouse, you begin to consider a career change.

You consider returning to school to study nursing. You considered taking extra classes to earn a certification to get a job promotion. You cried out at night – "What to do God? How will I manage? How will it work out? Do I continue working this good paying job especially in this terrible economy or do I make the decision to pursue my dreams, my wishes, and my desires." You are afraid to take the risks that are associated with starting your own catering business or consulting company. Even worse – you do not know who to contact, what to do, or where to start.

In my private psychological practice, I have also met clients who have been knocked off course due to an injury on the job that results in intense, unyielding chronic pain. When I meet these clients, they are in need of medical and therapeutic treatment to substantially reduce their pain to more tolerable levels so they can return to work or just improve their quality of life. Unfortunately, in many cases, they are unable to return to their former employer or they must learn a new skill or trade. These individuals are unsure of what to do or where to go. They spent years working in one field and that is all they know. They do not want to learn a new job! Unfortunately, circumstances are forcing them too. But now what? Where do they go?

A MONKEY WRENCH IN YOUR PLANS

There are definitely different variations in our entire story, but one thing is a common denominator: we all feel as though we were knocked off track due to some life event throwing a monkey wrench into our plans. What I have been through or what you are going through is not exceptional. Life can be unpredictable, harsh, and unrelenting. It can knock you off your feet, throw you curve balls and cause you to strike out of the game. As a result, you feel frustrated because you doubt that you will ever achieve your purpose in life or live a normal life. Truth be told, the once optimistic, motivated, goal-oriented person that you once were has now become a pessimistic, doubtful, and depressed individual. We have all been there, and we can all give a testimony or two of unfulfilled dreams that have been put on hold because of the game of life. Playing the victim, and saying "always me, always me" does not help. It just keeps you feeling depressed and hurt about your life situation. Pick yourself up, dust yourself off, and let's move on.

One cold, rainy Saturday morning in January, I was on the phone having my usual morning conversation with my sister, Tonya. My sister is a triple threat. She is brilliant, beautiful, and successful. At the age of 30, she is nearly finished with her PhD in Urban Policy and Planning. Probably by the time you are reading this book, she will have graduated and begun taking over the world! In our conversation that morning, my sister was not on top of the world. Instead, she was beating up on herself for not being done with her doctoral degree. She was disappointed that at the beginning of her doctoral program she "spun her wheels" working with an advisor who did not mentor or push her correctly or to finish her doctoral program on-time or to gain the skills necessary to become a researcher with a career in academia.

Tonya blamed herself for not heeding the advice of her classmates, which was to find another advisor so she could get the proper mentorship to graduate on time. In our conversation that morning, she was crying and dwelling on the mistakes she had made which knocked her off track. I told my sister to stop beating up on herself and to forgive herself. Beating up on yourself is ineffective and it serves zero purpose. It only keeps you in a state of feeling defeated, sad and frustrated, which further cultivates feelings of inadequacy and feeling like a failure which thwart you from reaching your goals. I also reminded my sister the "mistakes" she's made that knocked her off course should not be viewed in the negative. Rather, I encouraged her to see that they have helped and are molding her into the woman she is today.

Tonya's mistake of sticking with the wrong advisor will eventually help her in the long run. It will make her a more sensitive advisor to the needs of graduate students she mentors in the future. In the midst of her sobbing, she was unable to wrap her mind around how this circumstance was going to make her better in life. Sometimes when you are upset and emotional your judgment becomes clouded. It is hard to see things from a different point of view because you are upset. It is helpful to talk to someone who has been where you are, and can support you through your moment while listening and offering sound, trusted advice when necessary.

In fact, contrary to what you probably think, it is normal to get knocked off track. When you get knocked off track, avoid walking down memory lane with statements of "Should of, would of, and could of..." Also, avoid making negative statements about yourself, such as "How stupid was I to allow that mistake to occur!" Instead, forgive yourself for getting knocked off course, attach the jumper cables to your "dead battery" and jumpstart your life.

The Bible says in James 2:17 (NIV), "Faith without works is dead." Deep down, you have faith that you are capable and smart and able to accomplish anything. Without works, though, how can it come to life? It is never too late to discover, cultivate and fulfill your God-given purpose. Yes, you can have the career that you always wanted and create the life that you want to live. I am sure of this. The Word of God, in Jeremiah 29:11 (NIV) says *"God has plans for you. Plans to prosper you and not to harm you. Plans to give you hope and a future. Then you will call upon me and I will hear you."* As my pastor, Marvin E. Wiley of the Rock of Ages Baptist Church loves to say, "This is a power-packed scripture pregnant with possibility!!"

❖ When you read Jeremiah 29:11, what does it mean to you?

❖ What do you think God's plans are for your life? Jot down a couple of things you believed God has revealed in your spirit about his plans for you.

NO DREAM IS EVER TOO BIG OR SMALL FOR GOD

Please realize that God's plans are not to destroy us. Au contraire, mon frère! His plans are to give us hope that our future will be sound and prosperous. Take comfort in the fact that He is in charge. No purpose or dream is ever too large or small for Him. We must continue to persevere through the trials and tribulations. Through it all, the door slamming, injuries on our jobs, poor advisors in life and school, and rejection letters, God is still in charge! We must forgive our mistakes and remember that our purpose in life is real. The reason why your purpose is real and not imagined is because God wants to use you in your respective area of expertise as a platform to be a blessing to others in our families, communities, and churches.

You have continued reading this book because you can relate to what I have written. With the purchase of this book, you have taken the first step in jumpstarting your life and pursuing your purpose. My hope is that as you read this book you will understand the patterns in your life (fear, negative self-talk, or lack of motivation) that prevent you from realizing and living a purpose filled life. Through this book I will support you on your journey of exploration. I will be your GPS navigation system to help you understand your purpose in life. I will give you tools that I use with my clients and push you to believe in yourself. I will ask you tough questions because I believe you need to be aware of what knocked you off course. I only ask that while reading this book, you remain open, honest, and brave to take this journey with me and that you want to arrive at a better place in your life.

Embedded throughout this book are real life personal stories of individuals, including me, who triumphed over life challenges and fears to pursue and achieve our dreams. Allow our stories to inspire and motivate you to stay focused and achieve your dreams. I believe you will get there. Once you have arrived, you will have a testimony to give to inspire others to do the same thing.

This book is designed as an interactive study guide that will allow you to take notes in the margins and throughout the book as you discover the hidden talents that will ultimately make your purpose in life more real and salient. Take advantage of the discussion questions embedded throughout the text to challenge you to think critically about your wants and needs in life. This book will challenge those of you who may already know their purpose to re-ignite that vigor that has been dormant for so long to restart your engine, your life. At the end of this journey your destiny, purpose, and the essence of your being will be real.

Step 1

Identify Your Talents, Abilities, Gifts & Skills

As a child I had a knack for being creative. I loved to write short stories about things that interested me. In elementary school, I wrote stories about making new friends, the joys and pains of having siblings, and spending hot summers in Mississippi at Big Mamma's house. I continued to dabble in creative writing when I started junior high school.

In the 7th or 8th grade, I put my twist on a debacle that happened in American politics. I wrote a short story about two American presidential candidates of who were competing in a spelling bee. My teacher, Mrs. Spearman, was so proud of my work that she invited me to read it to my class. Standing before my classmates, I was a nervous wreck at as the words spewed from mouth. As I continued to read my story, it felt good to see my classmates and teacher enjoy my work. What was even more special was that my teacher shared the story with our school principal, and it was included in our school newsletter. At that time I did not know I had a gift for creative writing that I needed to cultivate and nurture. In the 7th grade, I was focused on other things in my life such as sports, boys, and friends. It never dawned on me that I had a talent waiting to be discovered. Writing was something fun that I thoroughly enjoyed.

Unfortunately, another 10 years passed by before I lifted up a pen to delve back into creative writing. Why did it take so long for me to return to writing? I am not sure. But what concerns me the most is what we have in common. You, too, had a wonderful talent and dream that you abandoned. It was years before I wrote again. I penned my first children's book while I was in graduate school at the age of 25, and I published my first short story about being blessed with a wonderful dad shortly thereafter. After a brief break to write my doctoral dissertation, I resumed writing. I confidently believe that one of my talents in life is to write inspirational stories or self-help books for adults and fun, yet relatable stories for children and adolescents to read. Living a life full of purpose and passion is exciting and calming.

Another talent of mine that I have been blessed, that of being a helpful, empathic, and understanding psychologist. I have been fortunate to attend workshops and seminars and to pay for extra training to cultivate my craft. It has paid off immensely. I counsel, guide, and help thousands of children, adolescents, adults, couples, and families whose livelihood has been affected by crises, conflict, and confusion.

Being able to provide counseling to others is my ministry and a gift from God. It is my purpose. I do not do it for the money because money will never make you happy. I have a passion for inspiring others. If I did not have a passion for what I love, I could not work 10 to 12 hour days at times tending to others' needs.

If you do not have a passion for your current job, you are not living a purposed filled life. Why are you wasting energy on things that leave you unfulfilled? Yes, I understand there are bills to be paid. Your family needs to be provided for, your kid needs braces and you need money to pay the mortgage. Gas prices are sky high at over $4 a gallon in some parts of the country and as a result food prices are also increasing. Yes, you need money! I understand. There comes a time, however, when life is about more than getting paycheck. It is about being fulfilled and passing on a legacy to your children that is greater than just earning enough to make ends meet.

Creative writing and helping others are just a two of my many talents, and I truly believe that I have many more embedded inside of me that I intend to extract like diamonds in a mine. I strongly feel my talents are part of God's divine purpose in my life which is to live a purpose and passion filled life where I strengthen and encourage my fellow brethren to use their God given gifts to have a positive influence on the lives of others.

❖ What are your TAGS (Talents, Abilities Gifts and Skills)? Please list them below.

❖ What are you great at doing or getting done? Please list them below.

In Matthew 25: 13-20, the Bible tells of a man who gave three of his trusted servants different talents or money to invest and grow. Two of the man's servants quickly invested their talents, watched it multiply and grow, and pleased their master. The third guy dug a hole and buried his master's talents. He did not invest it and watch it grow. His master was displeased with his actions and took his talents and gave it to the man who earned the most investments on his talents.

❖ What are you doing with the talents God has given you?

❖ Are you investing them to reap more or are you burying them because you are afraid to take risks to reap rewards?

❖ Would you want God to take away a talent he has given you or even worse, give your talents to someone else because you are afraid or maybe too lazy to use it?

Hopefully, after discovering your talents you will understand that your talents should be used for God's glory, to help others, and should not to be hidden. Your talents should also make you an income so you can live comfortably on Earth and be a blessing to others. Creating wealth and being R.I.C.H = (Residual Income

Creates Happiness) could be a financial blessing to others, and it should not be viewed negatively. As a business owner, one thing I have learned is that yes, it is good to offer pro-bono services to help others on occasion, but people should pay for your worth. Your talents are worth every penny!

I recognize that as you read these words you may be protesting, "I do not know what are my talents!" In addition to not knowing what are your talents, you may be asking, "Who am I? Am I a wife, mother, friend, or underrated employee? Am I a husband, father, son, or an overworked and undervalued team member?"

You may feel guilty, uncomfortable, or uneasy focusing on yourself. Maybe you have been trained since you became a parent to give up your dreams and wishes to focus solely on your family. That is what a parent does - you do not think about yourself, rather you focus all of your energy and resources on the needs of your child. And if you do not put your child first YOU ARE SELFISH! Have you been told by others that you are selfish for thinking about yourself? Maybe you have told yourself that you are selfish? You feel that your main goal is to work a nine-to-five J.O.B., which means you are which means you are JUST OVER BROKE, only making enough money to pay a few bills and provide for your family. You never have enough money for vacation, to put in savings, and to save for retirement.

Or maybe you feel that it is too late to worry about discovering and cultivating your purpose. Listen: embedded in that BELIEF is a lie!! It is never too late to live a life full of purpose. You are more than just a busy worker bee working the graveyard shift 6 days a week, slaving at machines that could cut off your finger or worse potentially end your life because of one mistake. You deserve to do more than just make ends meet. You should not miss out on fun times with your family because the only available job is an overnight shift that requires you to sleep during the day and work at night while everyone else is attending barbeques and other family gatherings. There's inherent purpose in your life, and I commend you in advance for taking the steps to know your purpose.

Additionally, you may think you are not ready to embark upon the journey of self-discovery because you do not have the time to invest. My question to you is can you afford to not invest in discovering your purpose? Each day you work long hours or late nights for a company you are investing in someone else's dream. In this book I am challenging you to invest in yourself. Take the necessary classes to advance your career. Invest in hiring a counselor or coach who can help you identify faulty patterns in your life from achieving your dreams. Invest your finances so you can prepare for retirement. Invest in Your Dreams, Hopes, and Wishes. Not someone else's.

Think you cannot afford the investment? We make time and find money for those things we think are truly important, those things that distract us from how unfulfilled our lives are. The hair dos, the new shoes, the cars, the clothes, the nights out on the town that we use to fill the void left in our lives by a lack of true purpose.

Your children need to see that their parent lives a purpose filled life so that when they become older, they have a great example of how important it is for a person to discover their purpose. When they see you working at it, they also are more likely to connect that living a purpose filled life contributes to happiness, peace of mind, and in many cases financial security and stability for yourself and others. If we chose not to show our children this example, it can contribute to them jumping from job to job where they always feel tired, rundown, and broke.

So I implore you to make the commitment today to invest in yourself!

My Commitment Card

I commit to making my purpose, my dreams, and my future a priority in my life.

I commit to being courageous as I discover and uncover patterns in my life that have prevented me from achieving my dreams.

I commit to not hiding my talent from myself or the world.

I commit to showing my children and family the benefits of living a life full of purpose.

I commit to applying the principles taught in this book to achieve my dreams.

_____

Signature & Date

Now look up to the heavens and say out loud to both yourself and to God, "I know MY PURPOSE IS FOR REAL! I have made a non-negotiable decision today to no longer hide my talents, abilities, gifts, and skills. I have made the decision today to let go of all unhealthy relationships that stifle my growth and development. I will start my own business, return to school to earn my degree or to get specialized training to move up the corporate ladder. I will contact a mentor to cultivate my talents. I have made a non-negotiable decision to be an example to my current or future children and grandchildren how to live a purpose filled life!

Step 2

Discover & Cultivate Your Purpose

There are some who enjoy marching to the beat of their own drum. They live life by the seat of their pants and always look for the next daring challenge. Why? Because it is fulfilling and provides them with an adrenaline rush that keeps them going. Then there are also those who allow life to happen to them because they have this internal belief that their fate is controlled by someone else, which fosters a sense of helplessness in their life. When you feel helpless and hopeless, you resign yourself to believing that you have no control over what happens in your life, and you believe that everyone else but you are destined to be important or to have some monumental impact on the lives of others.

My hope is that while you are reading this book, you will operate with the belief that you want to leave an indelible mark in the world. Your life and legacy are determined by you and not by the decisions or beliefs of others. Your purpose is your own. Your parents do not determine your purpose. Your past does not dictate your future. You will create the life you want to live because you recognize that happiness and fulfillment start and end with you. That is, you recognize that you are the only one in control of your life. Whether that mark is your name in neon lights on Broadway in New York City or having a larger impact in your family, community, and social circle, you want to leave a permanent mark on the world.

I am not a gambling woman, but I would bet that lately you may have spent a considerable amount of time questioning what makes you unique from others and why God has placed you on this big, beautiful, green earth. Well God has placed you on this earth because he wants you to discover your purpose to do his will. This time of self-exploration can be characterized as eye-opening and enlightening. You will learn more about who you are, what you like, and how you are destined to have an impact on the life of others. For many people, however, questioning one's purpose in life is not a pleasant process because of their difficulty pinpointing the meaning for their life. Oftentimes this process is accompanied by feelings of being overwhelmed and frustrated in part due to the amount of time that it takes and depth of introspection one must journey through to discover your God given purpose.

In the previous chapter, you understood that you have many talents, but you are uncertain of how those talents translate into your purpose. Further, feelings of frustration tend to emerge because we live in a microwave generation where we want to know it now. When I say we want to know it now, I mean we want to know what our life's purpose was last week!!

We actually want to press the fast forward button on the blue-ray disk player to the point in our lives where we are actually living out a purpose filled life. For many of us taking the time to figure out our purpose or in many cases re-discovering our purpose can be a painful process, and we would rather just get to the end where we our living a purpose filled life.

RUSHING THROUGH LIFE

When I was in graduate school I was under tremendous stress in my program to conduct research, to teach, and to train to be psychologist. To alleviate this stress, I would often go to 6pm evening prayer at my church to hear God's Word to calm my nerves. Before I began to pray with an elder of my church, I'd often express my frustration with life and made statements such as "I wish I could just press the fast forward button and have it all - my career, family, and a wonderful home." I frequently found myself making these statements because I did not like the journey God was taking me through to cultivate my purpose. Specifically, I was drained from the heartache, headache, and disappointments that I was experiencing from failing tests, not meeting my own expectations in a timely manner to complete my program, and struggling with being a broke graduate student. Through prayer I was able to release myself from the microwave mentality of needing to fast forward through my journey to discover and cultivate my God given purpose. What I soon found out that my failures and pain were part of necessary learning experiences often orchestrated or allowed by God to help me become a better psychologist in order to assist my future clients who will be dealing with the same stuff in life.

Do you struggle with having a microwave mentality thought process? Are you uncomfortable with the journey you are taking? Do you want to work in a field so badly that you impulsively jump in and out of your lane trying to get what you thought you wanted in life? For example, are you always jumping from one job to the next, looking to make more money only to be laid off from your new position within six months?

I once completed a psychological evaluation on a man who had 15 jobs over the past 5 years!! His impulsiveness and the need to feel important or fulfilled in his career had him jumping from one job to the next and it was affecting his marriage and his family. He would read about a certain job or field and often felt that is what he should be doing in life. He sometimes will spend hundreds of dollars to enroll into a training program prior to pursue the job only to quit the job after 6 months to a year because he realized that he was in the wrong career. Although he was learning a lot, he was steadily losing money and wasting time. His indecisiveness and frequent mindset shifts caused conflicts within his marriage. For my client, I had to help him realize what I think you are coming to terms with now.

"A man who stands for nothing, falls for anything."

In my client's case I had to help him understand there is meaning to his life and to pursue only those opportunities that fall in accordance with his purpose.

If you feel as if you have those same urges, consider talking to God about releasing you from the mindset that you need to always jump on the next big opportunity without thinking through the impact it has on your life and family. Additionally, consider talking with a professional counselor to help you understand exactly why you cannot stay put in one position and to provide you with tools to help you feel comfortable with pursuing the career of your choice.

THE UGLY GREEN MONSTER - JEALOUSLY

Another major reason why self-exploration is unpleasant is because it can produce envy and resentment. These feelings usually emerge as we are aware of family members, friends, and others who have seemingly understood their purpose with little problem. We see that person on TV, we read about them in newspapers, we visit their website and buy their music, yet we are frustrated that that person "has made it" and you are trying to scale your own heights. Here's a piece of advice: You often never know what another person has had to endure in order to get where they are in life. Try hard to avoid thinking that the other person had it easy. Many times we just see the finished product and assume the road traveled for them was easy and short. We have all heard the saying "Walk a mile in my shoes." What that essentially means is that you do not understand what I had to go through in order to become the person that I am today, until you have walked a mile in my shoes. You do not understand what I had to go through in order to become the person that I am today, until you have walked a mile in my shoes. You do not understand the late nights I had to stay up in order to get that proposal together to get that new job. You do not understand the time that I spent away from my family grinding to get to this point in my life. We are all guilty of this. We just see the final product and think that person just floated into that position, but usually that is not the case. The proverbial blood, sweat, tears, money, long hours, and lack of sleep have all have gotten them to this pinnacle point in their career, and it is our job to do the same to get to that pinnacle point in our career.

Maybe you have a close cousin who has a great career that she loves and travels for her job, and you cannot understand why you are still looking for a $12 an hour job. If you do not believe that you can turn your brown, dry lawn into the same lush green grass that she has (that is, if you do not believe that you can have these same opportunities and more), you will dwell in the house/ attitude of resentment and envy, and you will never turn your brown grass into a luscious green lawn. Fertilizing, planting and cultivating seeds are necessary to get your lawn lush and green. Dwelling on what others have or questioning whether the road was easy that someone else has taken in life is essentially not helpful. Not only will you not realize the blessings standing prostrate in front of you, but it may cause you to miss what future blessings God has in store for you. Unfortunately, your feelings of envy, sadness, frustration, and disappointment do not go away over night. Rather, they can linger around for some time until you finally make the decision to discover, cultivate, and fulfill your purpose.

So what is your purpose? Why were you created? What goals, aims, or intentions have you set for yourself? Is your goal or purpose in life to earn a paycheck every two weeks? Or are you determined to make a difference in someone's life? Are you challenging yourself to do more with your life or are you just settling for status quo?

I hear you protesting, "Dr. Tiffany, I don't know my purpose or my reason for my existence! How do I discover my purpose? Who do I need to talk to? What questions do I need to ask myself? What steps must I take to cultivate my purpose?"

There are many different roads you can take to discover why you exist. One road to discovering your purpose is to reflect upon the things that give you pleasure in life in order to leverage them into an income generating job or business.

We often experience pleasure doing a variety of interesting things. For example, what provides me pleasure is spending time helping people with challenges they are facing on their jobs or at school, or in their personal life with their families and children.

When I was in high school, I met with an advisor, and she and I were able to do some research to find out what career fits my personality. Surprise, it was discovered that I was best at being a helper. If you are not in college or working with a mentor, ask yourself, when you are doing things for your family and friends, what fills your heart with joy? When are you at your happiest? What inspires you the most? Is it when you are baking cakes, pies, and cookies for family gatherings? Or is it when you are helping people organize their homes or lives, sort out their complicated finances to help them complete their income taxes to earn a refund from the government? Or maybe you are filled with such joy when you minister to youth about the goodness of God and how he's blessed you despite your wayward ways. Whatever fills your spirit with pride, makes your heart jump, and gives you a joy is a clear indication that is probably an area to cultivate towards your purpose.

Another way to discover your purpose is to reflect upon talents that others have noticed in you, but you have just dismissed as talk.

For example, if you have a beautiful voice and others are always complimenting you on how far it can take you, but you have been reluctant to pay for studio time because you have a family and mortgage – maybe this is your time. Or if others have complimented you on how you are such an amazing stylist/fashionista and you have considered opening and running your own boutique, this maybe your opportunity.

What compliments have you received about an amazing talent that you have, that you dismiss as a talk? Write about it below.

As I mentioned a little earlier, discovering and cultivating your purpose, sometimes involves talking with a counselor and taking a career assessment test such as the Strong Interest Inventory to determine what personality characteristics you have that will fit perfectly with your new career choice.

Now, we are going to do a quick exercise. Everyone has seen or read a job description before. A job description is a "snapshot" of a job. The job description needs to communicate clearly and concisely what responsibilities and tasks the job entails and to indicate, as well, the key qualifications of the job – the basic requirements (specific credentials or skills) – and, if possible, the attributes that underlie superior performance. I want you to write a life description to see if you would be a qualified applicant to be hired to live that life.

MY OPRAH MOMENT

Another way of determining your purpose in life is to reflect upon the people who you admire the most and why? I admire and look up to a lot of important people in the word. I look up to Oprah Winfrey. She has her own production company, magazine, television show and television network. She is an actress, philanthropist and does her best to uplift the human spirit. When I think of Oprah, I do not think of the amount of money that she has. I think of how she has and continues to touch the hearts of so many people and has a positive impact on the lives of others. When I think about Oprah it inspires me to reach for unknown heights, to be a better person who continuously gives back to others. It pushes me to further grow my business so I can provide jobs, help others reach their dreams, and use it as a platform to raise awareness about topics and matters often afraid to be talked about.

I frequently tell this story to many people about my God Wink (God bless Squire Rushell!) that I, too, one day will have an inspiring life similar to Oprah. In May 2002, the day I graduated from Northern Illinois University, my family took me out to eat a very nice restaurant in downtown Chicago. As we stopped our car in front of the restaurant to go into, lo and behold guess who was standing right there on the sidewalk and just came out of the same restaurant? Yes, it was Oprah Winfrey!! My sisters and I screamed "Hi Oprah!" She graciously said hello as she waited with a friend to get in their car.

To some, that was a just a celebrity sighting. Big deal. But to me, that was a sign from God, an omen of what is to come. Yes, one day soon I will have my own television show. Yes, one day soon I will have my own magazine. Yes, one day soon I will have my own radio show. Yes, one day soon I will make others rich and famous. And yes one day soon I will have a positive impact on the lives of so many. It is possible. Look at Oprah!

I know I am not the only person who aspires to operate on an Oprah Winfrey level. When I walked into the office of my web developer, on his wall was a beautiful picture of Oprah, a one million dollar bill, Mercedes-Benz automobiles, and other goodies. He was having an Oprah moment and thinking big. Several months later, I went by his office to have some changes made to my website, and he showed me his new book. He was so proud of the work that he's written he stated he wondered how he could get Oprah Winfrey to showcase it on her show. For a few minutes we looked on her website to find information about how to submit an article to her. When we finished working that day and when I left his office he returned to looking through her website.

Maybe you are not an Oprah fan. That really is not the point. The point is for you to think about the person whom you most admire, and what about them makes them important to you? Are they a trailblazer in their respective field and you undoubtedly believe that you can do what they do? What characteristics do they have that you deem invaluable to you starting your life and career?

Recognizing there is a need in the market for a product can also help you jumpstart your life and career. How many times have we watched some infomercial and thought, "Man, if only I would have created that!" Or, "I know that my idea will generate so much buzz to help me launch my business!" If there is an area in business that you know is sorely lacking your skill or expertise maybe that is an area which God is telling you that you can carve your nitch into and make a name for yourself.

Now that you have a clear indication of what you are interested in or maybe you have already known your purpose from the beginning, but you have been unsure of how to get back on track to cultivating that purpose. Before we embark upon getting you on track, I challenge you to write out your life vision as to what you want in life. The Bible says in Habakkuk 2:2, *Write the vision and make it plain on tables so that he may run that readeth it.* If you do not write your vision for your life, how will you know the actions you should take in order to see it come to past?

Step 3

Overcome Anxiety & Past Disappointments

"*Our deepest fear is not that we are inadequate. Our deepest fear is that we are powerful beyond measure. It is our light not our darkness that most frightens us. We ask ourselves, Who am I to be brilliant, gorgeous, talented and fabulous? Actually, who are you not to be? You are a child of God. Your playing small does not serve the world. We were born to manifest the glory of God that is within us. It is not just in some of us. It is in all of us.*" – *Marianne Williamson*

What are your deepest fears that are holding you back from living a life full of purpose and passion? Are you fearful of being brilliant, successful, talented, and accomplished? Do you talk yourself out of attending networking opportunities to meet new people because you are anxious about what others may think of you?

You may not believe this – but it is normal to be anxious at times! Anxiety keeps us on our toes. It motivates us to perform better so we earn that promotion on our job. It causes us to study for long hours at night to ensure that we earn a good grade on a test. Anxiety also functions as part of our body's self-defense radar because it alerts us with signals (i.e., pounding heart, sweat, raised hairs on the back of your neck etc.) that we may be in dangerous or harmful situations.

Although anxiety can have positive functions, it also can interfere with your life's purpose because it can paralyze and prevent you from viewing yourself as successful beyond measure. It can cause you to feel uncertain, confused and disoriented as to the direction you are supposed to take in life. For example, you may want to move out of your current city or state where you were born and raised. You know there are better opportunities awaiting you if you head South, go North or head out West. God has revealed to you in your dreams, and whispered it softly in your ears, "GO! Trust me. I am God. It is your anointed and appointed time." The fear of leaving your comfort zone, keeps you stuck. Stuck in a dead end job without opportunity for promotion or excelling. It retards your personal growth and development because it keeps you dependent upon others for emotional, spiritual, and financial support versus branching out on your own develop those survival skills that will ultimately give you confidence that you can handle any and all situations you encounter in life.

SELF-FULFILLING PROPHECY

The origin of your anxiety may be rooted in deep insecurities and a negative self-esteem. Maybe you grew up in a home where you were never told you were gorgeous, handsome, talented, intelligent or creative. Maybe you were never told that you could be anything that you set your mind to. When you made mistakes, you internalized your errors as a reflection of your lack of ability. At the start of a new task, you approach it with trepidation and hesitation.

You frequently beat up on yourself and make self-deprecating statements such as, "This is too hard. I cannot do this. I am worthless. I won't be successful." An unhealthy self-fulfilling cycle emerges because you start to act like you are unworthy of success. Unfortunately, that energy is then emitted into the atmosphere and others interact with you and pick up on those vibes. They do not sense your confidence, success, purpose and passion and you are passed over for promotions, positions, and your motivation and confidence slowly erodes and declines. This cycle happens all too often with many of my clients. They begin to play small. They forget they were blessed with talents. They only see the failure, disappointments, and shame. They hide in the shadows of others and secretly wish they were living a different life.

THE JOURNEY YOU ARE TAKING IS IMPORTANT

In many cases, both women and men are anxious about the journey to uncover their purpose in life because they are afraid of change. We are all creatures of habit who enjoy routines. When our routines or daily life are suddenly changed, we can develop anxiety become we do not know what to expect.

Earlier today, I had in my office a wife/mother who has been married for over 15 years and suffers from depression and anxiety. This mother, named "Carrie" (the details have been changed to hide the client's identity) has a supposedly ideal family with two healthy children and a hardworking husband. Carrie is great at arranging parties, making arts and crafts, taking care of her children, and staying connected to love ones. She is unhappy with the state of her life. She feels like a failure and quitter because she has not done more in life in terms of pursuing a higher degree, keeping the pounds off, and having a life outside of her family. Carrie is in a rut.

Carrie is unhappy with life and wants her life to be better. She stated that many times she was presented with opportunities to challenge herself to be successful to fulfill her dreams, but she engaged in self-sabotaging behavior because she felt that she wasn't worthy to have such a good life. In our conversations, I taught her how to recognize when she was engaging in self-destructive behavior such as not applying for job opportunities where she could use her talents to make extra money, cancelling appointments with academic counselors at a college, and overscheduling herself to the point where she did not have time to do anything else. I taught her to view her gifts and talents that included having a compassionate heart and wonderful caretaking skills as blessings from God that should be shared with others.

Over the next several months, we addressed the constant stream of negative thoughts that robbed her of her self-confidence, caused her to view herself as inadequate, while placing others on a pedestal, and kept her awake at night. I had her view success not in terms of material things that we possess or watch others splurge on or consume on TV, but as a legacy that she can leave her children. I also had her measure success in small accomplishments until she felt empowered to move onto larger tasks such as starting and finishing a semester at the community college.

DO NOT FEAR CHANGE

Many individuals' stories are similar to Carrie's. They want to achieve their dreams, be successful and live a passionate and purpose driven life. They are afraid to start the journey because they fear it will cause dramatic changes in their lives. Here's a piece of advice – do not fear change. Change is not harmful. Again, scripture in Jeremiah 29:11 makes it clear: "*I know the plans that I have for you. Plans to prosper you and not to harm you. Plans to give you a hope and a future.*"

Do not become so set in your ways that you miss out on prime opportunities to grow and learn new skills that will help you to evolve into a better person. Do not get comfortable with the status quo and allow life to pass you by because you are afraid of change. Think about it: companies have to change over time to stay competitive and to attract new customers. Those companies which do not change or evolve are eventually run out of business or are bought out by their competitors because they have not kept up with the competition. In the past ten years, companies such as Circuit City, Blockbuster, and Borders, to name a few, have closed their doors because they have not kept up with change.

Fearing change almost kept my best friend, Ericka, from leaving her corporate job to pursue a career that she loves. Ericka was a successful Human Resources Manager at a midsize company. Her job included a wide variety of perks, including bonuses, travel and all of the new electronic gadgets companies try out to make their staff more efficient. All of that was fine and dandy, but Ericka was unhappy with her life. She worked 10 to 12 hour days at her job and had few opportunities to spend quality time with her young son. In her heart she wanted to return back to school to get an advanced degree that would allow her to be in a career where she felt happy, fulfilled, and enjoyed interacting one-on-one with people. Unfortunately, a fear of quitting a well-paying position and returning to life as a "broke college student," struggling to make ends meet to provide for her son kept her stuck in her career. To Ericka, the fear associated with leaving a secure job with benefits kept her working long hours and very stressed.

On a cold, snowy day in Chicago, Ericka and I were having one of our usual hour long phone conversations about life and she stated, "Tiffany, I cannot do this anymore. I cannot keep up this pace. It is killing me." I knew something of the toll it was taking on her, as I had not seen Ericka in several months because of her hectic work schedule. Sounding frustrated and tired she stated with finality, "I am going to give my resignation letter to my department chief." I wasn't shocked at her decision to step away from her job. She always felt that her dream job was a career where she helped others maybe as a teacher, nurse or a day care operator.

On the one hand she recognized it was a blessing from God to have a wonderful, well-paying job but she also understood that there is a season for everything. The experiences that she obtained from this position were invaluable and will certainly help her in any other career in the future, but she was keenly aware that her season in this position had passed and that it was time to achieve her dreams. Ericka realized that her purpose in life to be helpful to others was most important and finally seemed attainable.

She slowly developed a newfound confidence that she was going to be successful. She accepted that the road was going to be tough, and financially difficult, but she knew she was going to be successful and happy in the long run. I shared with Ericka that I was happy that she was regaining control over her life, but wisely encouraged her to have a sound exit plan that included the following: saving at least 6 months or more of her salary to ensure she had enough money to meet her monthly expenses; find income from a part-time job; and finally enroll in a community college to take classes training her to pursue her dreams.

I can proudly say that my best friend overcame her fears and has not looked back. Ask yourself, is your situation similar to Ericka's? Do you wholeheartedly believe that your life is destined for something greater than your present job or career? Are you fearful about leaving your job? Are you afraid of change?

When we are faced with the unknown (What would my life be like if I move away, pursue a talent or interest of mine? Will I fail? Will I prosper?), a lack of answers binds our ability to step out on faith and believe that it will all work out in the end. We also become fearful of how others will perceive us for pursuing an interest or idea. Others' perceptions can stifle our growth because we are too worried about how others perceive us.

STOP WORRYING ABOUT WHAT OTHER PEOPLE THINK & LIVE FOR YOURSELF

In life we should not be concerned about what others think of us. Consider this: if Oprah Winfrey worried about everything people said to or about her, she wouldn't have been one of the first African American women to launch her own TV network. If Kelly Clarkson or Rubben Studdard worried about how ex-host of American Idol, Simon Cowell, thought about them, they would have never won the competition or better yet, they would have never auditioned.

Over the summer, my sister, LaKeisha, and niece, Keeara, and I took the train to the Taste of Chicago. As we and maybe sixty or more people including four Chicago police officers were waiting for the train to take us home, a young man in his 20s took out his guitar, amplifier, and microphone and started his own concert on the train's tarmac. He sang some oldies but some goodies. It was amazing; his voice was powerful and beautiful, and he genuinely sounded wonderful. What was so fascinating about his performance was this man did not care whether I, Chicago Police Officers, or others perceived him as silly for performing in a subway tunnel. He continued to bellow his heart out and entertained us. He recognized he had a talent that he needed to cultivate and show the masses. He also probably recognized that many before him, some unsung talents, received their start playing for others in public places, and this led to their discovery by those who moved them forward in the music business.

I know, I know, I hear you protesting, "Dr. Tiffany, I do not have confidence like the man you saw. I am too shy!" Listen, you are no different from the man we saw. Do not let fear inhibit you. Let go of your fears and pursue what you want. If you are concerned about what others will think or say about you, realize that people will respect you more for pursuing your dreams and talents than for being fearful and hiding them. Who knows, we may see this man in another 1 to 2 years with his own record contract, and it was all because he had the guts to ignore others' perception of him and pursue his God-given talent. Who knows, I may see you in a few years on television singing to your fans, or I may taste your wonderful food or desert at a pastry shop, or I may wear one of your designs on a night out on the town.

OVERCOME PAST DISAPPOINTMENTS

In addition to anxiety and fear of change, we often let past disappointments stoke anxiety within ourselves to the point that we are afraid to pursue our passion areas. Disappointments are a part of life and we are unable to avoid them. I was disappointed in myself for getting arrested for fighting and getting kicked out of school. However, I did not dwell in that disappointment because I knew my value and self-worth. I knew that I made a mistake and that I needed to pick myself up again, brush off the hurt, and work harder, smarter, and better in the future. I also forgave myself for making that mistake and future mistakes (Yes, you will make mistakes in the future!).

You have that same bounce back power embedded inside of you. You may have been unsuccessful at school in the past, let yourself down by having a child at an early age, or engaged in illicit behavior such as dealing or using drugs or gang banging, but you have bounce back power embedded in you. In order to have that bounce back power work at its best, you must forgive yourself for the self-inflicted wounds or missteps you have taken. Stop beating up on yourself and let those wounds heal.

Everyone has made mistakes and fallen short of the glory of God. I have learned early and I teach my clients this all the time, we have all made mistakes, but it is how you handle the mistake is what really matters. Think about this, our current president has admitted to cocaine use in his youth. In his memoir, *Dreams of My Father*, Barrack Obama spoke about the poor decisions he made in his earlier years. What is so amazing about him, though, is that he always knew his self-worth and pursued his dreams all the way to the White House.

THERE IS NEVER A RIGHT TIME TO BEGIN – JUST START YOUR JOURNEY

Okay, I hear you protesting again. "Dr. Tiffany, I am waiting for the right time to pursue my passion, my purpose filled life. I want everything to be perfect and in order before I embark upon my journey." Then let me give you another piece of advice, there will never be a perfect time to do anything. Absolutely you should plan ahead to make sure you have your "ducks in a row" before you make a life changing decision. There will never be a right time to make room for discovering and cultivating your purpose.

The age old saying is true "You make time for what you want to do or for what you want to have." If you want to be in shape and lose weight, you must make time to exercise and eat right. If you want to live the life of your dreams, have freedom to start your own business, create your own schedule, and to be your own boss, you must make time to invest in yourself. Do not wait for any erroneous signs such as trumpets sounding or for opportunities to land on your doorstep. Time is of the essence and each day you wait to pursue your purpose is a day that keeps you further from living a purpose filled life. Each day that you invest in discovering and cultivating your purpose gets you one day closer to living the life you deserve.

THIS LITTLE LIGHT OF MINE – OHHHH – I AM GONNA LET IT SHINE, LET IT SHINE, LET IT SHINE, LET IT SHINE!

Do not be frightened by the potential of your light. Do not be afraid to let your light shine. Rather, let it shine brightly. Let it illuminate in the sky and in the life of others. When your bulb starts to flicker or dim out, change it. You are too close to achieving your dream to let darkness cloud your light.

Step 4

Get Your Life in Order!
Minimize Distractions
and Get Organized

Eliminating people, places or vices that distract us from focusing on the prize is extremely important to achieving your dreams. Intuitively, one would conclude that minimizing distractions in one's life is one of the easiest things you can do to ensure that you stay on track to fulfill your God given purpose and to achieve your dreams.

In my private psychological and coaching practice, many of my clients are not even aware of the people, places, items or events that usurp their time and deplete them of their precious cognitive resources needed to pursue and achieve their dreams. Additionally, many of my clients fail to realize how time is such a precious commodity that if it is not used wisely, you will never get it back. It is gone forever. The reset or rewind button that works great on your Blue Ray DVD player cannot be pressed to get that moment back in life.

Adolescents chronically fail to realize that time is a precious commodity. Teenagers believe they are invincible, immortal creatures with ample time in life to play and postpone living to their potential. They erroneously tend to believe they have all the time in the world so they do not need to focus on school, getting good grades, going to college, or their future. Their parents, friends, guidance counselors, and others caution them that their "light switch" called reality will eventually turn on, and when they finally realize that they have wasted so much precious time on unyielding things or people, they feel lost discouraged or confused. Failing to realize the magnitude that every breath that you take, each minute and day that goes by, can never be returned to you is a travesty. You must determine what is usurping your time and energy and preventing your dreams from coming to fruition.

I often have my clients complete a verbal exercise where I ask them to identify what eats up their time and resources. I ask my clients, "What are the roadblocks to you achieving your goal? Are you wasting your time surfing the internet and updating your status on a website? Are you wasting time in an unhealthy relationship or working a job that does not give you skills you can leverage to grow professionally? Are you still associating with friends that do not have the same mindset as you? Are you wallowing in self-pity about the failed mistakes that you have made? Or are you just plain old lacking motivation?"

Based on their answers, I encourage my clients to implement modest to moderate easy changes in their life and routine to give them additional time to maximize the chances that they stay on track to reach their goal. Once they have implemented those easy changes and they have some success under their belt, I then push them to eliminate more challenging distractions out of their life until they have successfully neutralized the barriers to achieving their dream.

In this chapter we will discuss some of the top things that I have identified in my clients that have distracted them from living a purposed fill life. We will also uncover distractions in your life that steal away your time and energy. I will also give you strategies and proven techniques to help you eliminate those things that will distract you from your purpose while helping you become more organized in life.

However, before we embark upon that journey, have you fully considered what is distracting you from reaching your purpose? Are some of the things that are distracting you, those things I named a few moments ago? Or are there others or a combination of things from my list and things you are aware of. If so, please take a few moments to list them below?

SOCIAL MEDIA DISTRACTIONS

Facebook, MySpace, Linked In, and Twitter are all wonderful platforms of social media that do an amazing job of keeping us connected. These websites allow us to share stories, pictures, and music with family and friends, they keep us abreast of what are the latest trends in American pop culture, music, and politics and they keep us up-to-date on what are favorite celebrities are doing and talking about. I have opened accounts on many of these websites and have spent endless hours updating statuses, checking tweets, leaving messages on other folks' pages, and pressing the "like" or next button to look at pictures and listen to music.

My goodness! I have connected with many individuals that I had not seen in over a decade on Facebook. I truly enjoy seeing pictures of those individuals and their families, as well as pictures of myself hanging out with family and friends. I have also befriended individuals, networked with, and learned about many new business endeavors through these networking sites. All of those are good things. One of the downside to using these social media outlets is that one can spend too much time being unproductive and too little time pursuing productive projects that will have more life benefit than just being an electronic gossip monger.

I am not just on my high horse or soap box here. I, too, have fallen victim to the social media bug. Instead of putting for 100% effort to build my practice, I spent time looking through pictures, reading updates, and chatting with friends. So after running my private practice for a year, I realized that I needed to deactivate my social accounts in order to refocus my cognitive resources on what mattered most in my life, which was having a successful business to generate income to sustain my lifestyle. (I have since reactivated some of my accounts once I got back on track to building my business, but I am much more cautious of the time I spend on them this go 'round.') This morning I even posted a status claiming "It is time to return to my A+ game because mediocrity sucks, and I know that I am not a mediocre person." This status was meant as a plug for this book. I learned to make those outlets serve me, and not the other way around.

I am not outright demanding that you deactivate or delete your accounts to these websites. Rather, I am suggesting that you assess whether the time you spend on them is benefitting you or is keeping you from fulfilling your purpose. Here are some tough questions to ask yourself: 1) When you wake up in the morning, do you first pray, meditate, or plan out your day OR do you log on to your social media account and leave a message telling your friends and family "Good morning." 2) Do you make more status updates, upload pictures, or play games versus researching programs to apply to, studying for class, or spending time with your loved ones? If you answer yes to either of these questions, you may be spending too much time engaging in these activities. You must make the decision today to better discipline yourself in regards to the precious time you allow yourself to waste engaging in activities that have no real bearing on your personal success.

Social media are not the only websites that distract us. Shopping has gone cyber! Opinions are all across the Information Superhighway! What is it getting us? How are these things benefitting you? Spending hours surfing the internet to visit your favorite clothing stores, gossip websites, and political blogs can equally deplete your energy and resources which could be better used to towards fulfilling your God given purpose. Do not get me wrong: everybody surfs the internet from time to time. It is as much a part of our life as the television, telephone or radio. If you are always surfing the internet or sending and responding to emails, when do you have the time needed to pursue your passions, dreams, and aspirations? Twenty years ago we would have asked if you are always watching your favorite TV shows, how will you stay on track to cultivate your passion area, your purpose? It is the same thing.

COUCH POTATO

Sitting on the couch to watch endless hours of TV in the evenings after work on every weekend truly is a major distraction worth discussing. According the Nielsen Company, the average American will watch approximately four hours of TV a day. That equates to 28 hours of TV watching a week and 9 years of watching TV by time you turn 65 years old. Wow, that is a lot of tube viewing! What could you do with an extra 28 hours a week? What degree could you pursue or what extra training you could receive during that time? The noises you hear from the TV for the most part do not inspire or motivate you to get your life in order. Rather, situation comedies, reality shows and dramas seldom are examples of using time productively.

For almost two years, I disconnected my cable service and only watched TV sparingly. I used the time when I disconnected my cable to get back into reading books, hanging out with loved ones, and working on my growing my business. It paid off because I was able to kick my addiction to the tube. Yes, you can get addicted to watching television! The TV allows us not to focus on our reality and we develop a bad habit of not dealing with our own issues; instead we focus on how messed up others' lives may be. Get off the couch, turn off the television, and take back your life. It is ridiculous how we make others millions watching their TV shows, but we do not invest in ourselves to be more knowledgeable, to be more financially stable and comfortable, or to be happy.

EXCESSIVE PARTYING

So maybe the Internet, TV, or social media are not big distractions in your life. Great! But that does not mean there are not other things that are distracting you. I have a client who for the past five months has been looking for a career in the field that he got his bachelor's degree. My client is smart, helpful, and great at what he does. He sent me his resume and cover letter to critique with hopes of securing a position in his passion area. As I reviewed his resume, I noticed that he has not received any up to date certifications or trainings that will make him marketable as an employee. Yet, this client desperately wants to work in his passion area. So what is keeping him from expanding his knowledge base and earning a higher level of training – he is! My client loves to go out every weekend to the clubs and party. When you party almost every Friday night, wake up late Saturday afternoon, you do not have the time or energy to pick up a class at the local community college or library to learn an extra trade. So in my client's case his Friday nights are keeping his skills stagnant.

Partying and hanging out with friends at social events, the club, and bar is not a problem. It is fun to get out and let your hair down from time to time. When that happens to be every weekend or more evenings than not, when do you have enough time to focus on your craft? When do you focus on you? How can you expect to earn good grades in that challenging Accounting class in order to gain acceptance in a solid MBA program if you are leaving your brains on the dance floor? If you are always out partying and you get home late, when do you have the extra time to work on that certification you will need to get your resume to stand out or to garner you more attention or clients to expand your side business?

Minimizing distractions is not for the faint at heart because you must be disciplined, dedicated, and determined to avoid doing nothing on the couch in order fulfill your purpose. In my opinion, minimizing distractions is one of the hardest things a person must do in order to achieve their goals. There is always some tempting website to surf, status to check, and party attend. If you are not disciplined and allow distractions to permeate your life, then you essentially steal cognitive resources and precious time you need to get back and stay on track.

UNSUSPECTING BILLS AND BEING BROKE

You may have never considered this one – but unsuspecting bills work wonders to distract you from your purpose. Those can be the ultimate distractions. For example, how many of us have gotten a large bill in the mail that we owe from a hospital or doctor's visit for a sick child or dental visit due to a chronic toothache? Or how many of us have gotten into a car accident and what we thought was minor damage in fact amounted to a couple of thousand dollar repair bill? Unsuspecting bills or expenses can be unnerving especially when you are trying to make a dollar out of fifteen cents! Even though most people view unexpected bills as a part of life, they can fry your nerves; steal your cognitive and emotional energy and joy as you try to find the funds or borrow money to pay the bills.

Lack of money in the bank account to pay the bills may serve as unintended reminder that you are broke and may encourage you to put your dreams on hold until you are able to pay off your bills. What is interesting is that most of us will never have enough money in the bank like our favorite celebrities to pay off bills as they come while we continue to pursue our interests. We still cannot let unintended expenses or bills thwart our focus. Acknowledge that it sucks to have to pay the bill, but do not beat up on yourself for having made the bill, call up the bill collector and arrange a payment plan, then move on to focusing on your purpose. If you always allow yourself to become unnerved or sidetracked by bills or expenses, you will be stuck in neutral and not be able to move forward in life.

THE METEORIC RISE AND FALL OF TIGER WOODS

There are a variety of professional athletes, music stars, and thespians who have had to minimize distractions and spent countless time on their craft to be successful. Let's examine some of those who have minimized distractions to excel in their respective fields. I think we can all learn a valuable lesson by reviewing Tiger Woods' life. Tiger Woods is one of top of the athletes in the world with countless endorsements from major corporations because he won nearly every major golf tournament. This is a man who was extremely disciplined as a child athlete; practicing and perfecting his swing shot since he was two years old to become the number one golf player in the world. In my research about Tiger Woods, in order to accomplish so much in his short life and to achieve to such heights, he had to accumulate at least 10 thousand hours a of swinging the golf club over and over and over again to perfect his golf game. He had to forgo excessive partying for endless practice.

However, Tiger Woods eventually got off track. He suffered a huge blow to his personal life when he lost his mentor and his best friend which was his father. According to Tiger, he lost sight of his personal goals and became easily distracted and swayed by acquaintances that did not have his best interest at heart and he made bad decisions. Before you know it, his life started to crumble all around him. He lost his wife and family, multi-million endorsements, and a lot of corporate support he had come to take for granted. His personal life essentially imploded. As incredible was his meteoric rise as a beloved American athlete, he, too, was not immune to being knocked off track and do not you forget that neither are you. Distractions serve to stifle you from accomplishing your goals.

LACK OF TIME MANAGEMENT

I would be remiss if I did not talk about one of the biggest things that can distract anyone from working towards their goal, which is lack of time management. Time management involves reducing your stress by focusing on things that matter the most to you and eliminating other burdens on your day. Time management goes beyond keeping a day planner that outlines what you must do for the day and crossing it off the list as you go. It involves setting up and keeping routines for your day so you can easily anticipate what you should do next.

Time management also involves allowing a little extra time or wiggle room in your day to recover from unexpected mishaps to you routine which occur; not allowing unwanted things to frequently disrupt your routine. Additionally, it involves eliminating the conversations with a girlfriend gossiping so you can go to bed on time to get up an extra hour earlier on Sunday to work on the tasks you did not accomplish the night before or additional goals you have set for yourself. Time management involves telling people "NO, I am sorry I cannot help you today because I already have plans to stay in to study for my big Accounting test." Or, it requires you to plan how much time you have to devote to completing a task to ensure it is a quality project and not rushed through.

Time management and procrastination go hand in hand. Individuals who have difficulty with time management usually struggle with procrastination. They put off completing homework assignments, projects, chores, and running errands until the last minute because they convince themselves they have enough time to get the task done. In many cases they erroneously believe that they work better under pressure when they wait to the last minute to write a paper or complete a project. They soon realize they have underestimated the amount of time that they actually need until it is too late. The unexpected occurs (i.e., a child gets sick, car breaks down, an emergency happens at the office all requiring immediate attention, or your dog gets hit by a car – this happened to me, oy!!) and they do not have enough time to complete both tasks.

Unfortunately, the project with its approaching deadline then suffers as the individual rushes to finish the task with enough time to spare to start and complete an entirely new task. As you may suspect the quality of their work performance is poor. It is barely enough to get them a passing grade on an assignment. Individuals who procrastinate frequently underestimate the amount of time they need to run an errand or get prepared for work. Consequently, they speed to get to their final destination driving recklessly like a mad man down the highway placing theirs, yours and my life at risk.

Finally, procrastination due to a lack of time management promotes a spirit of mediocrity. According to Merriam-Webster dictionary, the definition of mediocre is 'of moderate or low quality, value or ability or performance, to be ordinary or so-so. Who wants to be an ordinary, so-so, person? Think about the past week in your life. Were there any days in which you practiced poor time management skills? Did you procrastinate to complete a project?

Last week I had a client who has poor time management and struggles with procrastination contact me to reschedule her Friday afternoon appointment for earlier in the day. She stated that she had two papers due on Saturday morning and that she needed to complete and having an earlier appointment after she got off work would allow her to work on the papers. Of course the first thing that I am thinking in my mind is "I hope she's not waiting until Friday to start these papers." So, I rescheduled her appointment from 3pm to 12pm.

On Friday I walked into my waiting room to welcome my 12pm appointment, who we will call Charlotte. Unfortunately, Charlotte was late. In fact she was 20 minutes late to our appointment. When she finally rushed into the waiting room she was completely apologetic. I asked her why was she late especially since her job was only 10 to 15 minutes from my office and she responded, "Dr. Tiffany I have horrible time management issues."

"Is that so?" I asked with a chuckle, looking at my watch.

"I know, I am sorry," she said as she caught her breath. Charlotte stated that she called off work to finish her papers and that she drove 45 minutes from her home to our appointment. She also stated that she should have had one of her papers nearly written before the start of our appointment; when she woke up that morning she proceeded to go back to bed. "Why?" I asked. She stated she did not feel like getting up. She stated that she eventually woke up at 10am to get started on her paper which she worked on for an hour. Her family then woke up and she decided to run to McDonald's to get them something to eat. Of course, the line at the restaurant was long so when she finally returned home it was 11:30. When she finally left home to come to our appointment, she had to speed down the highway driving approximately 80 miles an hour to avoid missing the appointment altogether. Before I continue with her story, let's pause here to determine what mistakes did Charlotte make? What could she have done differently?

First, Charlotte admitted her papers were assigned over a month ago, but she kept putting them off because she felt entitled to some me time after working hard. As a result, she put off working on her papers until the last minute. Second mistake is calling off work to finish two papers. Save your days off for something important such as a celebration, sick child, or mental health day. Do not waste time taking off work in order to complete an assignment. What message is she sending to her child or her boss that she must call off work due to poor planning on her part?

Charlotte then stated that her daughter sleeps in the bed with her so she does not want use a separate alarm clock with a loud ring to avoid waking her daughter who has her own room and bed! Although rarely, but it does happen, she oversleeps her alarm clock. I recommended to my client to put her daughter in her own bed. She's too old to sleep with mommy and daddy and purchase a separate alarm clock which she places on the dresser farthest away from her bed. That would then force my client to get out of the bed to turn it off, which will help in waking my client up in the morning, and eliminate her ability to snooze.

Additional mistakes included not having breakfast items at home to prepare for her family. This is healthier for her family and it saves Charlotte time, energy, money and gas from having to go to McDonald's for breakfast.

Charlotte continued to say that she is always late to work every day even though her job pushed back her start time from 6am to 6:30am because she kept arriving to work at 6:30. I asked how her long was the commute from her home to her job and she stated approximately 30 minutes. She sets her alarm for 5:30am and she snoozes for 10 minutes or so until she finally gets up to take a quick 10 minute shower and get dressed. After getting showered, she quickly puts some street clothes, grabs her makeup and applies it in the car while she rushes to make it to work late.

I asked Charlotte what consequences has she faced for coming to work late. She stated that she had faced none. In sort of an astonished tone, I asked, "Really?"

Charlotte reiterated that she had never been written up for coming to work late. Even though she arrives late to work every day, she completes all of her work by the end of the day. Then I prompted her to think again. There were all sorts of consequences she was facing – some that were noticeable and some that were not. The noticeable consequences were the frustrating looks her co-workers gave her for arriving 15 minutes to a half hour late each day while they put for the effort to arrive on time. An additional noticeable consequence was that she was passed over for a position that she applied for because she lacked supervisory skills. Charlotte said she was frustrated that they denied her the position, but I challenged to her to see it from her employer's point of view. Why even allow an employee who consistently arrives late to work to supervise other employees? Why even allow her a chance to get earn those skills when she hasn't demonstrated in her daily work activities that she deserved it?

I also pointed out that Charlotte doesn't look the part of a supervisor. She arrives at work in jeans, comfy sweater, and flats, which is far from the look of a supervisor. Every day that she arrives to work late she was reminding her bosses that she was only equipped to be a mediocre employee and nothing more. As a result, she never gained more experience to get a better position, she was costing herself future earnings down the road, and she was teaching her two year old daughter the same unhealthy patterns. That is, waking up late, arriving to work late, and dressing like an employee and not like a supervisor was causing her to never get ahead in life.

Another distraction that truly deserves a chapter of its own is eliminating negative self-talk and engaging in positive thinking. This talk screams in your mind and thwarts you from believing in yourself. It convinces you that you cannot live a life of purpose nor achieve your dreams. In the next chapter, we will also discuss how negative self-talk successfully neutralizes your ability to remain focused on staying and keeping on track to watch your purpose materialize, and how negative self-talk paralyzes you when you are so close to running across the finish line and claiming your prize.

Step 5

The Power of Engaging in Positive Thinking

It is been said that humans think thousands and thousands of thoughts each day. What are we going to do today? What bills we are going to pay? We have thoughts about what we are going to cook for dinner. Many of those thoughts are generally harmless and do not influence your mood or how you feel on a daily basis. When your thoughts shift from "what I am going to do today" to "Why cannot I ever catch a break; why are things so easy for her and tough for me," is when your thoughts become harmful to your self-confidence and you can end up feeling defeated, upset, and dismayed.

Those types of thoughts tend to exist throughout the day and often become worse at night. The busyness of your day which served as a temporary distraction from those thoughts is no longer there. When you are in your bed, those thoughts can keep you up at night because you have not found a way to shut them off. They dash across your mind like a rabbit running away from a predator.

Did you know that your brain is the most active at night? Those thoughts that were running rampant all through the day now seep into your dreams and become so vivid that you are unaware if you are sleeping or still going through your day. You are unsure of when exactly you fell asleep. One thing is for certain, the same things you thought about earlier during the day are keeping you awake at night, thus causing you not to sleep soundly. You keep checking your alarm clock to see if it is time to get up. When you wake up in the morning, you may feel tired, worn, and exhausted because you never got 8 hours of good, continuous sleep.

You start your day with the same thoughts you had when you went to bed. The cycle never changes, days turn into weeks, and weeks turn into months of poor sleep. Occasionally, you get a good night of sleep if you take an over the counter sleep aid or drink a glass of wine, but you are afraid to do so on a regular basis for fear of becoming too dependent on it to fall asleep. Does this sound like you?

YOUR THOUGHTS ARE NOT YOUR ENEMY

Your mind, your thoughts and your emotions are not your enemy! It is vitally important that I emphasize that point to you at the outset because too often people feel so beat up by their thoughts and emotions to the point that they do not know what to do to change things. Some resort to unhealthy strategies to avoid those thoughts by numbing themselves with alcohol and drugs or worse trying to commit suicide because they believe that is the only way to get the thoughts to stop. If you are using some of these unhealthy strategies, do not grin and bear it or face it alone. Seek out help from a professional counselor who will get you through this turbulent time.

Others do not engage in such drastic measures to eliminate their negative thoughts, they avoid coming in contact or interacting with loved ones, friends, and others who may ask simple questions such "Have you found a job yet; what have you been up to lately?" or pass along the good news of others – "Have you heard so and so is moving to Atlanta because they just secured a $100k a year job?" because they trigger negative thoughts. So many of us are tired of giving the same old response to this question: "What have you been up to lately?"

"Nothing… just working – trying to make a dollar – same old same old."

As I previously mentioned, engaging in negative self-talk can successfully neutralize your ability to remain focused on your purpose. Negative self-talk will make you think that it is too late to turn your life around because you are too old and inadequate. Negative thoughts will have you up at night crying, angry and sad during the day. These thoughts will make you feel utterly defeated and worthless. In this chapter, I will teach you how to replace those destructive, irrational thoughts which can cause overwhelming emotions that vex your mind and spirit by consistently engaging in positive thinking.

YOUR ATTITUDE DETERMINES YOUR ALTITUDE.

We have all heard the saying that *Your Attitude Determines Your Altitude.* Essentially what that statement says is that your disposition, your mood, your attitude, whatever you choose to call it, will determine how far and how high you will excel in your life. It will open doors that wouldn't otherwise open for people who are unpleasant, crabby, and dejected. People will tend to listen to you more attentively, value what you say, ask for your help on a project they have or advice, and may be inclined to extend a helping hand to you, when you are someone they can connect with.

Unfortunately, when people have negative thoughts about their situation, their attitude or outlook on life is pessimistic, and they are unable to soar to heights as high as an American Eagle to accomplish their dreams. Their negative thoughts create a bad attitude which causes individuals to make bad decisions and choices, which results in a negative outcome, which further perpetuates a negative cycle. Conversely, positive thoughts can cause you to be in a good mood and having a positive mood can lead to good decisions and actions, which can result in positive altitude and outcomes for you.

IMPROVE YOUR SELF-CONFIDENCE BY BELIEVING IN YOURSELF

In order to change your attitude you must first start with improving your self-confidence. Self-confidence doesn't emerge overnight – rather it is a seed that you must plant, water and nurture and protect it as it grows. Self-confidence emerges when you believe in yourself. When your self-confidence improves, you are less likely to become rattled by the unexpected because you are certain that you can handle it. Also, a confident person doesn't shy away from challenges. They embrace putting in hard work and effort because they know it will pay off.

You must believe in the talents that God has given you, and know for certain that He did not give you those talents to hide them, but to use them to benefit or help others. Self-confidence grows when you experience success using your talents. Whether it is marginal success or huge success is not important. What is important is just trying and exceling at something that you are good at. Successive attempts in your talent area will boost your confidence and motivate you to continue to try again in the future which ultimately leads to success in life.

Once you involve yourself in activities that you know you can perform well at, it boosts your confidence so you believe you can handle larger projects in the future. For example, if you are considering going back to school to study nursing, it may feel overwhelming to enroll in college and take a full credit load. Start off small and only register for an easy, but slightly challenging class that you know you can handle its demands. Get used to the idea of returning to school, doing homework, taking tests, and juggling the demands of school and home life. After you have successfully completed the class and earned a grade of a B or higher, then take two classes next semester and apply the same formula that you used to past the first class to pass the next two. Too often people take on too many classes at once in the beginning because they think they are Superman or Superwoman and they can do it all, and they want to quickly get done with school. They do not get used to the change in lifestyle. They automatically assume that it will be business as usual. Unfortunately, they take on too much and wear themselves out face, eventually drop a class, and lose their confidence and mojo. What I suggest is that you build your confidence by taking your time and pacing yourself. Do not rush it! After you have successfully passed two classes with good grades then consider taking a full-time load.

ELIMINATE THE WEEDS OF SELF-DOUBT

Please realize that the weeds of doubt will grow to tell you that you cannot make it. They will steal your mojo and sunshine, and make life extraordinarily difficult for you. Do not get rattled. My mother, who is an avid gardener would recommend that you do not break your back bending over trying to tug, pull, and yank every weed from the ground each time you see one pop up. Rather, she would suggest that the best way to eliminate weeds is to be proactive and control their growth from the beginning by applying a two to three inch thick layer of mulch before the weeds even appear to deprive the weed of sunlight while preventing the seeds from other weeds from landing in your garden, germinating and growing.

I also recommend that you do the same in eliminating the self-doubt that grows to eliminate your confidence. Symbolically, grow a two to three inch layer of skin to protect your confidence from attacks of the enemy. God says the enemy will come to seek, kill, and destroy just like a roaring lion. Jesus says I pray that your faith does not fail during this time. I also pray that your faith does not fail during this confidence building time. Your faith must be the size of a mustard seed.

Protect your self-confidence by believing that you are the head and that you are not the tail. Believe that you naturally possess characteristics and skills (i.e., you are humble, can calmly handle unexpected problems effectively, an effective communicator, forward thinking, trustworthy and inspirational) of an effective leader that will ultimately help you become the lender to many and not the borrower. As a leader others start to believe in you and want to follow you because you are positive, friendly, and intelligent. They will seek you out and recommend you to their friends and family because they have witnessed firsthand that you are man or woman of integrity and Generosity. They will drive business your way which furthers results in positive outcomes which furthers your personal success.

Believing in yourself does not mean that you will look down upon others that have not gotten to the point where you are in life. When you thumb your nose at others or look down on others' problems, misfortunes, and mistakes, it provides you with a false sense of confidence which will not cushion the fall you take from your high horse when you realize that your poop smells too. Too often this is the biggest problem many people make. In order to boost their personal confidence and self-worth, they spend time dwelling on others' problems, talking about and making fun others, and comparing themselves to others who are less fortunate. The expense of others should not make you feel more confident in yourself. Rather, the best way to feel confident is to experience your own success and to revel in it.

Yes, you will encounter difficulties in life. We all do. Are they fun to go through? Of course not, and yes, they can be painful. Then what purpose do they serve? Why cannot life just be easy? You must have a test in order to have a testimony. They teach you the value of hard work and discipline. They teach you that "the best things in life are worth working for." Yes, life has been difficult, but you are not a victim – rather you are a victor. Indulging in the victim role even for a moment may garner you sympathies from others; however, it prevents you from taking responsibility from improving your life. Eliminating the 'victim' mindset also allows you to come to terms with the fact that life is not easy, and it helps you to recognize that the final chapter has not been written in your book. There is still more to come and more waiting for you.

AFFIRMATIONS

I am a magnificent, wonderfully created, child of God who was placed on this big, beautiful, green Earth not to take up space, but to have a positive impact on the life of others.

I am incredible and I can do all things through Christ who strengthens me.

I can accomplish all that I set my mind to do.

Life is tough, but I am the victor and not the victim.

What I have just written are some of the affirmations that I say to myself on a daily basis to encourage myself when I get frustrated, feel overwhelmed, or I need to stay encouraged to finish a project that I am working on. We have all heard "power lies in our tongue." You have the power to use words to speak things into existence. As a child we have said things such as "Sticks and stones may break my bones, but words will never hurt me." As the young folks would say, "Do not get it twisted – words do hurt! We must watch what we say to ourselves and to others.

Affirmations can be short, positive, encouraging statements that we say to ourselves to uplift ourselves in dark moments, to keep us focused on our inner goals and dreams, and to thwart off thoughts of defeat and giving up. Affirmations can be comforting hugs, thumbs up signs, high fives, smiles, head nods, winks, pat on the backs, pat on the butt, fist bumps and chest bumps to illustrate to ourselves and to others that you are on track and doing a great job hanging in there especially since the road we may be traveling on is not paved.

Affirmations work by undermining irrational, dysfunctional, negative, pervasive thoughts which affect your behavior, attitude, and mood and may keep you up at night. They challenge those thoughts at the core by altering how you view challenges that lie ahead, while reconfiguring your brain to frame challenges not as insurmountable, impossible or problematic, but as doable, achievable, and rewarding. Daily use of positive affirmations creates a lasting fissure between those old thoughts and future outcomes. With daily use, you can start to see a change in yourself. Your thoughts become calmer, easier to believe, and less stressful, and you feel better about yourself and your future. You do not just view tomorrow as another day, another dollar to make to pay the bills. Rather, you will start to view tomorrow as another day that inches you closer to your ultimate goal. You tend to expect the best, and to interact with the universe as if you are having a good day.

Affirmations should be repeated throughout the day. They should be written down and posted in high traffic areas in your home for you to see. They should be written on small index cards in bright marker and taped to your mirror in your bathroom. They should be posted in your cubicle to remind you of better things to come in life and at work. Not only do I believe this, I practice this belief.

When you walk into my office, you will notice inspiring words in beautiful frames on my walls. I purposely decorated my office that way. I wanted to send my clients subliminal, positive messages while they sit in the waiting room or in my office receiving treatment. There are messages of HOPE, LOVE, FAITH, HARMONY, DREAM, IMAGINE, INSPIRE, and PEACE. Whether my clients hear it from me, they see encouraging words posted directly in front of them. I have them complete an exercise where they write positive affirmations to challenge the negative thoughts they say. I will encourage you to do the same. On the affirmation card, list five affirmations that you can say to yourself every day.

My Affirmation Card

Affirmations can be short, positive, encouraging statements that we say to ourselves to uplift ourselves in dark moments and to keep us focused on our inner goals and dreams. Please write five affirmations below.

1. _____

2. _____

3. _____

4. _____

5. _____

_____
Signature & Date

SURROUND YOURSELF WITH POSITIVE PEOPLE

As a child, my parents would always tell my siblings and me to watch the company that we keep. They always would say "Birds of a feather flock together." Essentially what they were trying to communicate to was, if we hang around people who are up to no good, failing classes, misbehaving at home, then we were likely to learn and duplicate their bad habits. Even if we did not necessarily pick up their bad habits, people will likely assume that since we were cavorting with children who got into trouble, and that we, too, were problem children. So my mother would say, "Do not hang out with Suzy from down the street. She's a sassy child and her head is not on straight." This was my mother's way of saying, "Something is wrong with that child!" Hearing statements like those, I quickly learned that I should not give my personal space and time to everyone. Does that mean I only hung out with the snobs and nerds? Absolutely not! It just meant that I needed to hang out with people who were also like minded and going somewhere in life. Coming from the near west side of Chicago, of course I knew of classmates who were involved in gangs or hanging out with the wrong crowds, but I steered far away from them and made lasting friends and connections with individuals who thought like me or had similar values as my family.

In college, I did the same thing. I did not party all the time or hang out with other students who were spending endless hours getting drunk at night and then missed their first class because they overslept. I hung out with individuals who were funny, smart, and motivated to succeed at the same time. Does hanging out with funny, smart, and motivated people mean that I had a boring college experience and missed out on a lot? Absolutely not! I enjoyed my college experience and did some of the same activities as children my age, I always remembered in the back of my mind what my parents said. "Spend time with people who are going somewhere and not stuck in the same position."

Now in my daily life I continue these same practices. I am a member of two awesome women's organizations that allows me access to the best and the brightest. At every feasible chance I get, I spend quality time in their face because they are innovative, stellar, sophisticated, polished, breathtaking, inspiring, positive, encouraging, and going somewhere in life. I try to be a sponge absorbing their life lessons and learning how to be a better person. Spending time with them truly inspires and motivates me to live a better life and to run a more efficient business.

I am in awe of these women's credentials and feel blessed to have their telephone numbers stored in my phone. They call to check in on me and to give me encouragement and advice when I have a difficult moment personally and professionally. They ask me to lunch to ensure that I am being mentored and to give me an opportunity for a sounding board when it is needed. They share their personal stories and testimonies that remind me to hang in there and not throw in the towel. They pass on leads about other business opportunities because they want to see me succeed in life. These individuals continuously make more deposits versus withdrawals in my life and I thank God for blessing me with them.

Who surrounds you? Are you the most successful in your pack of friends without someone close that you can admire? Are you hanging out with individuals whose thoughts are negative and whose mood and disposition are always sad which only bring you down? Are you involved in organizations or groups so you can interact with positive people and learn their tips to success, peace, and happiness?

MISERY LOVES COMPANY

Unfortunately, this saying (Misery Loves Company) is so true! People who are not happy with the state their life is in, tend to gravitate towards people who are in a similar position in life. Make the decision today to do an inventory of the ten people in your life who gets the majority of your face time, excluding your children – especially if they are young. Of the individuals you have named, what percentage would you classify as positive, uplifting and encouraging, and what percentage would you classify as mediocre – that is they do not encourage nor hinder your progress, and what percentage would you classify as dead weight?

Those you have classified as dead weight you should seriously consider removing from your "Fav Five." I did not say cut them out of your life because everyone needs a friend, someone they can call on especially in times of need. Scale back from calling them on a regular basis just to shoot the breeze or to play catch up; scale back from going to the mall, club, or bar with them all the time; scale back from hearing their same old sob stories every day. When you do decide to call to talk or to hangout, quickly change the subject when it goes back to the same old tired rhetoric. Set an example that you are looking for a friendship that edifies you, not a friendship that obfuscates your purpose and outlook on life.

POWER OF PRAYER

The effectual fervent prayer of the righteous availeth much. Fervently praying is the most effective way to communicate to God that you love Him, trust Him, and need Him to *show up, show out, and deliver a blessing* in your life. Praying is a positive and powerful way to move mountains, obstacles, and roadblocks out of your life that maybe too strong on your own to move. Prayer alleviates anxiety and stress that you may feel as you are getting your life in order because it gives a calming reminder not to sweat the little stuff that is bothering you. You do not have to sweat the little stuff or stay up at night because the Creator of the Heavens and Earth, a Spiritual being that is all powerful, omnipresent, in control of your life, and that He will work everything out according to His Will.

Is it in God's will to see you successful? Absolutely! Remember, the word of God says in Jeremiah 29:11, *For I know the plans that I have for you, plans to prosper you and not to harm you, plans to give you a hope and a future.* God wants to see you prosperous. He wants to see you succeed and do well in life. He wants the tests that you have faced in life to be a testimony to others that they, too, can overcome trials and be triumphant in life.

In order to be an overcomer, a victor and not a victim, to be triumphant, and to be successful at what you set your mind to, God asks for you to trust Him. In Proverbs 3: 5 & 6, He says, *Trust in Him with all thine heart, and lean not unto your own understanding. In all thy ways acknowledge him and he shall direct your paths.* Essentially, what God is telling you to do is trust him, to stop trying to figure it out because your understanding is limited in comparison to what his overall and masterful plan is for your life. He also asks for you to get on your knees to pray and acknowledge Him so He can direct your paths so he can get you back on the right track to achieving your dreams.

When you put your full trust back in God, the Word of God says to let your petitions be known unto him. It also says, in Matthew 7:7, *"Ask and it shall be given to you; Seek and you shall find; Knock and the door will be opened unto you."* Here's the catch, when you pray be specific about what you want God to do for you. If you want God to give you the strength to walk away from a job you hate to pursue your passion areas, then you must believe without wavering that

He will give you the strength and courage to leave while making a way for you to make ends meet.

Many days I have gotten on my knees and prayed over my offices and asked God to send me such an abundance of cash paying clients that my cup runneth over in ways that I did not have enough room to receive it. I have asked God for my business to grow in unthinkable, unimaginable ways. I truly believe the opportunities that I have been blessed with (my advice being showcased in magazines, local and national radio segments, pursued by major network to do TV, and a thriving business); the incredible people who have encouraged me and been a blessing to me; and the success that I have attained in my personal and professional life are solely because I have asked and believed without a doubt that God will always provide for me. Understand that the power was not in the eloquence of my prayers to God because in actuality my prayers were not eloquent! I truly try to keep them short, consistent and to the point. Rather, the power lied in God's ability to bless me because He heard my prayers and like my earthly father, He wanted to give me the desires of my heart, because they were within in His will.

The same applies for you, too! God wants to give you the desires of your heart. He tells us in His word, in Romans 8:28, *All things work out for good, for those who love the Lord and are called according to His purpose.* As you are reading this book, let me be one of the first to say or to remind you that you have been called according to His purpose. It will work out. You will see your dreams come to fruition. Will it be easy? No it will not. But as my parents always say, God does not put any more on you than you can handle. You can handle the pressures of life and what he has in store for you. Pray for strength. Pray for guidance. And Trust that He will never, ever forsake you.

If you are unsure of what to say when you pray to God, let me offer you one of my prayers.

Dear Heavenly Father,

Thank you for being a merciful, loving, and kind God. Thank you for your protection, guidance, and care all the days of my life. Even when I was lost, you have always been there by my side guiding me every step of the way. Thank you for never giving up on me. I love you Lord, and there is none like you. Heavenly Father, I pray in your son's Jesus name, that you will give me the strength and the courage to get my life back on track to help me achieve my dreams. I believe that my purpose is for real and that you have plans for my life – plans to prosper me and not to harm me. Father, when doubt or anxiety seeps in to make me want to give up, I pray your hedge of protection around me, and that I will have faith the size of a mustard seed that you will answer my prayers and help me to stay on track. Thank you for what you have done and what you will do for me in the future. In your son's Jesus name I pray, Amen.

Step 6

Make Sacrifices While Investing in Yourself

Now that you have discovered your purpose in life; identified and overcome anxiety and past disappointments; got your life in order by minimizing distractions and becoming organized; regularly engage in daily positive thinking and meditation to combat pervasive, negative thoughts that used to paralyze you from achieving your purpose; it is time to move on to the 6th step, which is making necessary sacrifices in order to see your dreams come to fruition.

I encourage all of my clients to make sacrifices in their personal and professional lives in order to see their dreams come true. On the surface making personal sacrifices does not seem like a difficult thing to do. We have all done it before in life in order to purchase something that we desperately wanted, to lose a few pounds "to look cute and in shape" in time for a summer trip, or to save money to pay off an outstanding debt.

The sacrifices I encourage my clients to make are not difficult. This process, however, can be challenging because the sacrifices must be maintained for an extended period of time. Furthermore, it can be challenging because sometimes individuals often do not receive the necessary reinforcement and encouragement and they give up out of frustration. Sometimes due to a lack of encouragement reinforcement, they give up erroneously believing the light at the end of the tunnel is not shining at all.

MY PERSONAL JOURNEY AND SOME SACRIFICES I'VE MADE

When I decided to become a licensed psychologist, I made the decision to go to graduate school for at least five years in order to earn my PhD after I spent four years in college earning my Bachelor's degree. I knew it wasn't going to be a cake walk and understood this process I was undertaking was going to be tough. Essentially I knew I was sacrificing my 20s, a time typically considered as part of your "glory years" where you get an entry level job, work your way up the corporate ladder, spend money on clothes and trips, party, date, and stay out late at night. Instead of living like a typical 20 something, I hunkered down and focused on my studies. I gave up purchasing the newest designer clothes, getting my hair done on a weekly or biweekly basis, traveling with friends to exotic places, the luxury apartment, and the new car. I also put on hold having a serious love life. Yes, I occasionally dated, but I found it truly difficult to focus on cultivating a relationship and school at the same time. My mother's oldest living sister, Aunt Margaret, words would ring in my ear when

I would hate feeling single. She would say "Baby, you have a lifetime to date and be married but only a heartbeat to focus on school."

Giving up cultivating a long term relationship was especially tough when friends would tell me their juicy stories about the men they were dating and the places they would go for fun and visit. But my aunt's words were comforting – as well as having a core network of friends in graduate school who were in the same position as I.

My entire 20's definitely weren't a wash! In terms of learning, I gained practical knowledge and experience from working in the school system as psychologist in training, teaching an undergraduate level course for three years at UF and then receiving a teaching scholarship at the University of Missouri at Columbia, and volunteering as a mentor. I honed my craft by attending and presenting at countless conferences, conducting and publishing research, writing my dissertation, and interning at a therapeutic school. Yes, I was disciplined and focused, but even during those years, I still took time out to smell the roses!

Smelling the roses for me involved going to the movies with friends, attending occasional gatherings at each other's home, conversations on the phone (my phone bill was a bit high!), inviting my friends and family from Chicago to come visit me in Florida, driving to the beach on the weekends to lay out in the sun, and occasionally heading to Orlando, Atlanta and Miami for big city fun! You must ask yourself a tough question; can you make and maintain the sacrifices for an extended period of time to reach your goal? Anything worth having is worth working for. I will also add it is also worth sacrificing for.

RECOGNIZE AND CELEBRATE
ACHIEVEMENTS

In graduate school, I learned to celebrate the little achievements that I made along the way because they meant I was one step closer to the light at the end of the tunnel. That is, I was one step closer to that seemingly elusive pot of gold. For example, at the end of each semester I would take myself out to dinner and treat myself to a day at the spa with a girlfriend. For major or even minor accomplishments during that time, I would call family and friends so they could congratulate and motivate me to hang in there and push on. There's nothing narcissistic about having others share in your glory. Your family and friends are your support team, your cheerleaders and you should want them to say "Job well done!" Also, at the end of the year, I would take a mini vacation and drive to the nearest big city to hang out with friends that another year was over. You must do the same. When you fail to reward your hard work and effort the sacrifices you make may seem like more pain and no gain. Too much pain will only undermine your purpose in life, may cause you to resent this journey you are traveling, and an unbalanced life will derail you from reaching your dreams.

My sacrifices did not end after I was done with my course work, conferred my PhD, and returned to Chicago to start my career. I had additional post-doctoral training to purse and to two major exams that I needed to take in order to call myself a licensed psychologist and a certified school psychologist. This process involved another two years of training and studying. Thankfully, this process wasn't as arduous as earning my doctorate, but there were a few more sacrifices I had to make, such as missing friend's parties because I had to stay up late to take a test.

Overall, from start to finish the process took 8 years of maintaining sacrifices to see my dream to become a licensed psychologist come true. I know this may seem extreme to you and your journey certainly may not take you 8 years to complete, but the point that I am trying to make is that one must make and maintain sacrifices for an extended period of time especially after they have figured out their purpose in life and set things in motion to see the manifestation of their purpose.

SACRIFICES YOU SHOULD NOT MAKE

Before we discuss the types of sacrifices that you should make in life to achieve your dreams, let's first discuss the types of sacrifices I *firmly* believe that you should not make to achieve success. Many people erroneously believe that in order to achieve success, and be the very best at what they do, they need to sacrifice personal pleasures such as sleep, quality time with their loved ones, friends and family, and the all-important occasional mental health day of relaxing around the house, or exercise time. And this is just not the case!

First, a drive to be successful should not cost you personal relationships with your family members, friends, and loved ones. Everyone needs family and friends to keep them grounded as they pursue success. When work becomes overwhelming and life becomes difficult, it is important to have people in your corner that you can talk to, laugh with, take your mind off the pressures of life when they are abundant, and keep you grounded as you become successful. Also, your family and friends become your cheerleaders, and they help you celebrate your accomplishments. Sacrificing these relationships in pursuit of a career because you think that is the only way for you to stay focus or to not be tempted to hang out or party is not the case. Friends and family are vitally important to maintaining your peace of mind, happiness and emotional well-being. We need them for our sense of belongingness, connectedness, and personal happiness.

A frequent gripe that I hear in couples counseling is "Dr. Tiffany, I supported my husband/wife returning to school. I believed it was a good idea. It would allow opportunities for them to seek a better job promotion which will lead to more income in our household for our family's sake. When they returned to school, they forgot about me, they forgot about our family. I am doing all of the work around the house. After class ends, when he/she comes home, they just get a bite to eat and go into the other room to study. I ask him/her to spend quality time with me, but they always have work to do. I feel alone, angry, and frustrated. I damn for sure did not sign up for this!"

But how do you maintain these relationships while pursuing success? Take a few seconds to reflect and write on whether you have done a good job at maintaining these relationships. And if not, what could you do to improve in the future?

Your drive for success should never be unaccompanied by watching your relationships suffer or your family suffer. Life is about balance, and I recognize for many that is difficult to do. There are so many things that demand your attention that it is hard to ensure you are spending quality time in or devoting attention in all areas. Busy, successful people must balance their desire to achieve professional and monetary success with their need for belongingness, connectedness and personal happiness.

To maintain a healthy relationship with your spouse or partner, your drive to success may involve getting up earlier than usual to get an assignment or project completed. Once the family is awake it is necessary to give them their fair share of attention and focus. It may also involve using your spare time in the evening wisely and not waste it watching television. Rather, you may split up some of that time to study for a test, and use the other half of the time helping your children with a homework assignment, talking with your spouse about how was their work day, or even cuddling in the bed. Or your drive for success may involve finding employment with another company that will allow you to pursue your professional goals, but will give you time in the evening to spend quality time with your spouse and/or children.

Letting your relationships with friends and family members suffer is unnecessary. They, too, have frequent gripes that you do not call any more, stop by to say "Hi!" or even hang out. You guys used to talk once a week, now they are lucky to get a ten minute call or an occasional text from you once a month. Yes, you will need to scale back from attending all of the family barbeques, friends' parties, and hanging out at the club so you can focus on your studies, your business plan, or earning that promotion at work. Remember, abandoning these relationships can be detrimental in the long run. Friends may not be so eager to come back around after you have reached your goals. It is not that they are jealous of your accomplishments because in many cases that is not true. Likely, they may feel so hurt by you cutting them out or not being accessible, they've moved on and learned to live life without you. Your pride may say "forget them, they weren't a friend in the first place if they left because I focused on me," but they were. Remember friendships are about reciprocity. If they are the only ones calling, inviting you over and giving, it is bound to cause the person to give up and move forward.

The last sacrifice that you should avoid making at all costs is sacrificing your personal integrity. If you are making that type of sacrifice, let me be the first to say **PLEAE STOP!** There's no need to cheat, take any shortcuts, undermine coworkers or colleagues, or step on others toes to climb the corporate ladder, to reach the top, or to become the best. It is important to know that you are worthy beyond measure. With hard work, perseverance, determination, and motivation, you will reach your goals. Never allow a person to talk you into doing these things; even if it takes you twice as long to reach measurable success, just appreciate the journey you are taking. It fosters a sense of pride, accomplishment, which you can then use to motivate you further to accomplish other goals.

SUCCESSFUL PEOPLE MAKE SACRIFICES

A well respected marketer and music executive believes "if you want to get to the top, you have to fall in love with the pain of hard work." The long and short of it: in order to be successful and to watch your dreams become a reality you must make sacrifices. If you ask any successful person how did they become the best at what they do; how did they achieve their dreams, I can almost guarantee you that most will say they never gave, up, were willing and eager to make some tough, yet positive sacrifices, and they believed in themselves and the goals they set forth in life.

Making sacrifices whether large or small did not matter to them. What mattered to them most was seeing their dreams come true. They also were not afraid of hard work, stress, and failures. Some people shy away from hard work. Some people tend to call these individuals or view them as lazy. It may not be that these individuals are lazy. It could just be that they never fell in love with the pain that it took to get to the top. Successful people have a love/hate relationship with pain. Yes, they hate how it makes them feel frustrated, overwhelmed and tired, but they love the pain because they know without the heartaches, headaches, and stomach aches from stress, pain, and hard work, they wouldn't be back on track towards achieving their dreams.

As I mentioned to you before, my sister, Tonya, is finishing up her PhD in Urban Policy and Planning. My other sister, LaKeisha, has quit her job at an orthopedic clinic in order to return to school to earn a second bachelor's degree, this time in nursing. Lastly, my best friend, Ericka, quit her job to return to school to become a physician's assistant. What these three ladies have in common is that they made sacrifices – large and small, personal and professional – because they realized their purpose and calling in life and they were determined to watch their dreams come true. On a side note – some of the people closest to me/that are in my inner circle – all have drive and ambition. It is true; birds of a feather do flock together! We need to be around individuals who are likeminded pursuing their dreams because it motivates us to stay on top of our game. If you are around individuals who do not want much out of life, how much further do you think you will get in life?

Each of the women I listed earlier cut out extracurricular activities that were unrelated to their goals, avoided or reduced contact with people who sucked up their time and resources from their studies, and/or they even quit their jobs that prevented them from focusing 100% of their energy and efforts on the most important thing to them – their purpose in life and dreams. They were and remain determined to give it their all – to become the best, to be successful, to be a winner and they weren't going to let anything stop them or get in their way.

Many of our elite athletes such as golf pro Tiger Woods, tennis pros Venus and Serena Williams, hockey legend Wayne Gretsky, ice skating phenom Michelle Kwan, basketball great Michael Jordan and countless others operate under that same mentality. They will tell you that they spent countless hours working out and practicing daily to become the best in their field. They often opted out of staying up late partying with friends to get adequate rest and nutrients to ensure the performed at an optimal level. They have made a non-negotiable decision to maintain these sacrifices for the long haul until they earn the coveted title as the "Best in the world." Even after winning a championship title or two, gold medal, or banner, they did not stop. They set the bar higher and continued to make the same sacrifices until they reach the next goal they've set. You should do the same.

Once you have accomplished your major goals, set another one and accomplish that one. Never stop raising the bar after you cleared that height. Keep pushing yourself to become the best in your field. Becoming complacent in life serves little purpose for teaching your children and family members that the value of hard work and effort does pay off. Also a spirit of complacency means you do not trust and believe that you are capable of doing more. You are not just a 9 to 5 employee. You are wonderful human being blessed with talents, abilities, gifts, and skills from God which should be used for his glory and to create a wonderful life for yourself. Have an attitude of more!

SUCCESSFUL PEOPLE DELAY GRATIFICATION

Sacrifices may seem quite painful to you in the moment because you desire to travel with friends and family members, buy the latest gadgets, toys, clothing items and shoes. Your desire to hang out with friends at parties is understandable! Who enjoys sitting in the house on a Friday night reading a book for class the next day. Since we were children, many of our parents gave in to our requests and we got the latest toys, clothes, and trinkets when we wanted them. In today's society the media teaches us not to delay in purchasing the next electronic toy or taking the trip of a lifetime. We are trained consumers and immediate gratification is pleasing to our senses. We are barraged daily with deal of the days that we cannot afford to miss, products to buy and consume to our hearts desire, and places to go visit.

Anything worth having is worth fighting for. Yes, you are in a fight for your life's purpose!! Do not view delaying gratification as a denial of fun and freedoms. Delaying gratification does not mean you have been denied from ever enjoying the fruits of your labor. Delaying gratification means you have a high level of self-control and can withstand caving into desires because you understand and respect the benefit of postponing these moments of pleasure to a time when you can truly reap the harvest you have planted. Celebrating and partying and living a good life too soon before you have put the necessary foundation in place to enjoy life on a long-term basis, is truly not the best idea. Realizing that you do not have as much in savings as you intended, you are living paycheck to paycheck, and you have not accomplished any of your goals and wishes in life, can be depressing. Why put yourself through that turmoil? Make the decision today to prioritize what is important - your purpose, goals, dreams and wishes or buying the newest electronic, attending a party, or taking a trip of a lifetime.

MAKE SACRIFICES BY CUTTING OUT THE FAT

A client of mine is a married father of three children. He stated in one of our sessions that he realized how his lack of a sacrificial mindset and difficulty with self-control were affecting his family and their future. This client regularly would shoot pool with the fellas at a local pool hall once a week to release some pent up energy. While there, they would order some wings, have a few beers, and shoot the breeze. Additionally, he stated that he was at the barbershop weekly getting his hair cut and beard trimmed, and once a month purchased the latest gym shoes ("sneakers" for my east coast folks!) or a video game. At first glance this doesn't sound like a big deal.

This client of mine worked in a factory and made $17 an hour. In my work with Larry(we are changing his name) he realized that he wasn't demonstrating enough self-control over his life, and was essentially living over his means, and did not really have anything to his name to leave his children. He was leasing his car, renting a house with his wife, and barely owned any stock in the company he worked for. Larry soon became frustrated with the life and legacy that he was leaving for his family. What he wanted out of life was to own property, return to school to be an independent contractor who could one day have his own construction company that he could get his children to follow in his footsteps and maybe leave the business to one of his young boys. By age 35 he wasn't making any moves in that direction.

Larry enjoyed hanging out with the guys shooting pool and having a good time, but he realized that the $30 to $40 he was spending a week did little towards saving for a home, returning to school, or getting ahead in life. Larry felt overwhelmed. He stated that he didn't have a master plan in life; he was just living. "Everyday sometimes feels like Monday." In our conversations, I shared with him that everything does not need to be spelled out in terms of how to get his business off the ground. That is putting the cart before the horse. He really just needs to get started somewhere and soon! And the amount of money that he was spending weekly on hanging out with the fellas, getting his hair cut and beard trimmed, as well as buying new toys would forever undermine his goal of leaving a living legacy to his children. Here is the kicker: Larry enjoyed spending time at home, and knew how to cut and trim his hair on his own. What would he miss?

Larry made the non-negotiable decision to scale back his spending habits. He sat down with his wife to discuss the plans for their future. They made a list of their goals they would like to achieve as a family and individually in the next five years. Together they decided to take ownership for their future, and started taking toddler steps towards leaving a legacy to their family. I purposefully put toddler steps, because baby steps would have been too slow. He was already a married, father of three so slowly carving out his plan was not going to be efficient. Larry trimmed the fat from his budget by scaling back hanging with his friends weekly, only bought his video game/ sneakers for big occasions such as his birthday or Christmas, and put the money he was now saving into a savings account. He also registered for one class towards his goal of becoming an independent construction contractor.

The changes Larry has made have helped him immensely. He's been able to save up money for a rainy day and retirement, his savings are growing and his relationship with his family is improving thanks to the time he dedicates to them. Most important, Larry feels he is moving forward, which is the first step in pursuing your purpose.

SOME NIGHTS WILL BE LONELY — BUT GOD IS WITH YOU

It is a lonely road at the top, and I can truly attest to this. I was the first in my immediate family to go away to college, the first to graduate, the first to get a PhD, and the first to own their own business. Along the way, I did not have many people to turn to help me figure out how to apply for college, scholarships, assistantships, and how to incorporate a business. The lack of people walking this journey did not scare me away. Rather, it motivated me to pave a path for my sibling, my nieces, my friends, and future children.

The road to the top is definitely far less traveled. There are few people who can relate to you on your journey that you can talk to along the way and the unpaved road is tiresome on your feet. You may question whether to turn back. When you pause to slightly turn your head and body around to see the road you have traveled thus far and to determine whether it is worth going back, you realize that you have come too far to turn back now. Continuing on an often bumpy, dirt filled road with twists, turns, and forks in the road that is not particularly well lit does not seem pleasant.

The journey is long and the staff that you are leaning on is the word of God. He's constantly whispering in your ear that he's the lamp unto your feet. He is whispering for you to trust in Him with all thine heart and lean not unto your own understanding, in all thy ways acknowledges him, and He will direct your path. He wants to be your GPS device or compass and point you in the right direction. As you are walking, He's turning the bumps and stumbling blocks in the road into your footstools.

You may feel weary and tired from the journey of discovering your purpose, and He understands that. In the morning, He renews your strength and gives you new mercies to continue walking to achieve your dreams. He places your name on the heart of others and they, too, pray for your strength and for blessings to be bestowed upon you. He gives you favor by sending good Samaritans along your path to help you on your journey especially when you are discouraged. These angels give you support, offer love donations, babysit or lend a helping hand and remind you that there are kind, decent people who care about you. No longer are you weary and neither are you faint. As you are walking, He gives you insight in which to reflect upon your life thus far, and to assess the necessary steps you must take to achieve your dreams. You have decided to stop imagining and dreaming about your purpose and being successful in life, and made the non-negotiable decision to invest in yourself and your craft.

MAKE A NON-NEGOTIABLE DECISION TO INVEST IN YOURSELF

Now that you are back on track towards living a purposeful life and watching your dreams come to reality, you must make a non-negotiable decision to invest in your primary cash cow which is You! The reason why it needs to be a non-negotiable, firm decision is because some people are afraid to spend money in honing their craft because they believe they can use this money towards other things such as paying off bills and eventually talk themselves out of wisely spending money on themselves. Investing in yourself often involves wisely spending money in a variety of modalities to continue to hone your craft and become great at what you do. If you do not continuously invest in yourself, your skills can become outdated. So the old adage is true, "In order to make money, you must [wisely] spend money."

As an entrepreneur, I am continuously finding ways to invest in myself and my business. While I am writing this section of the book, I am actually on a 15 minute class break. I am registered in a two year Neuropsychology certificate training program. Yes, I am addicted to learning! First, let me back track and explain why I am registered in another two-year post-doctoral training program after earning my PhD in psychology.

A few years ago, the field of education stopped testing children to diagnose learning disabilities and attentional disorders that affect children academically, behaviorally, and emotionally at school. A federal initiative called Response to Initiative (RTI) has mandated that schools do not wait until children are failing academically and provide immediate academic supports performing below average. In the past, schools would wait for progress reports or 1st quarter failing grades before requesting that a child is tested to determine whether they have a learning disability, and based on the test data obtained, recommendations are made to treat the learning disability. Schools now do not believe there is a need to test children; however, doctors and parents still request neuropsychological, psychological, and/or academic testing because they want the information they glean about their children from the evaluation.

Recognizing there was going to be an increased need for neuropsychological testing I invested over thirty thousand dollars in my business by going back to school to learn a new skill. Since taking this course, I have been able to grow my business and increase my profits by 40%! Is the course costly? Yes, but it is definitely worth every penny. No one can take the knowledge away from me. It goes with me wherever I go.

I have invested in my business in other ways. When I first opened my practice, I did not have much money and I was very selective in terms of what I wisely spent. While surfing the internet, I ran across a website called BlackExperts.com. The website allowed experts in every area you can think of to list themselves for others to learn about them on the website and possibly hire them as an expert. To list myself on the website cost $200. I decided to take the plunge and make the investment. Since I have been listed on the website as an expert in psychology, I have been approached by magazines (Jet, Parent Paper, Chicago Parent, and Black Enterprise Magazine), radio (Michael Baisden Show and WVON's Santita Jackson and Koolout radio show) and a major television network (ABC) and production company (Shed Media) which have led to more exposure and credence as an expert.

I have decided to invest in my business in a number of ways. I own a growing group psychological practice and we are based in the western suburbs of Chicago. Recently, my business was bursting at the seams, but we lacked a larger office space to accommodate our growing business needs. I decided to lease a larger office space for my therapists and me to spread out to see more clients. Acquiring a larger space involved doubling the amount of rent, getting more office furniture, and buying new software to accommodate my growing practice's billing needs which all cost more money. My business plan projects that we will recoup this investment and see it pay for itself and then some in the near future. Again, you have to spend money to make money.

My advice is to never stop investing in yourself. You are your greatest asset. Here are list of some best ways to invest in yourself.

1. TAKE A REFRESHER COURSE OR SEMINAR

2. GET A MENTOR AND/OR HIRE A COACH IN YOUR FIELD

3. GET EXPOSED TO MORE AND LEARN MORE BY ATTENDING CONFERENCES, WORKSHOPS

4. GET A WEBSITE AND BUSINESS CARDS TO PROMOTE YOURSELF

5. EXERCISE AND EAT RIGHT TO LIVE A HEALTHY LIFE AND ENJOY THE FRUITS OF YOUR LABOR

6. CUT ALL UNNECESSARY CREDIT CARDS SO YOU ARE NOT SPENDING MORE MONEY THAN NECESSARY

Step 7

Celebrate! You are Now Back On Track!

Celebrate good times, Come on! It is a celebration. There's a party going on right here. A dedication to last all year. So bring your good times and your laughter too. We are going to celebrate and have a party for you.
– *Kool & The Gang*

IT IS TIME TO CELEBRATE!!

When you were knocked off track from pursuing your dreams many, many moons ago, I bet you probably never envisioned that you would have the courage, tenacity, or intestinal fortitude to get life back on track so your dream can be a reality. You were knocked off track by a variety of things (i.e., becoming a teenaged parent, death of a loved one, legal infractions, self-doubt, fear, depression and anxiety). The pain of being knocked off track was a skeleton in your closet that you feared like Freddie Krueger. It was a black cloud draping over your life that was upsetting to think about. It was easier to just maintain status quo and focus on everyone else's problems, needs and wishes versus the needs of your own.

Emotionally, mentally, and physically it has been a long, winding, bumpy road back to redemption. God created you in his image, and you are now a victor and not a victim! Yes, at times you felt overwhelmed but you know for sure that you are an overcomer!! At times, you probably felt like giving up, throwing in the towel and saying it is not worth it. Or even worse – you thought you weren't worth it. But you persevered through trials, tribulations, heartaches, and headaches while taking this journey, fell in love with the pain of hard work, and hung in there. You chose to be a believer and not a doubter of what is to come in your future. That is worth celebrating! You are back on track!

What an amazing race you just completed! The most amazing thing about your journey is that you when you started out, you did not know your purpose. Looking back from where you started and where you are now in life – you can now rejoice that you have finally rediscovered your purpose in your life! What an awesome feeling to be confident that you are more than a mother or father (although that is one of the most important purposes in your life) or an employee at a JOB where you are **J**ust **O**ver **B**roke.

Go ahead and do your happy dance! Shout! Rejoice! Do not be shy. Go put on your favorite song and dance. Many people do not even know what their purpose in life is and you are one of the lucky few who do know and have made a commitment to get back on track to achieve your dreams. Oh what a mighty feeling you must have! Others may not understand your joy or praise, but who cares. You now are able to answer questions about who you are and your purpose – something that was truly difficult to do at the beginning of the book. Hallelujah!

By now you know the answer to:

1. What are my TAGS?

2. What are my values? What do I believe in and would like to spend my time doing?

3. What organizations, people, or causes can I use my talents to help assist their efforts?

4. What legacy will I leave my children and my children's children?

I commend you for following the steps outlined in the book, answering the reflective questions, and overcoming those adversities to reclaim your rightful place on this big, beautiful, green Earth. God sees how much you have dealt with to get to where you are, your faith has grown immensely, and He will reward you for seeking His face, trusting Him and living a life that he envisioned before you were born.

I know this is not the case, but for whatever reason if you have gotten to Step 7 and you are unable to celebrate finding out your purpose, then you need to go back and reread the beginning of the book about your TAGS and Discover and Cultivating Your Purpose. You may need to go back and reread the other chapters of the book to ensure that you continue to overcome anxiety that will creep up from time to time, understand how to minimize distractions, and apply the power of positive thinking daily in your life. The benefits of finding out your purpose and getting back on track are numerous, and you don't want to short change yourself by not knowing.

Undoubtedly, one of the biggest benefits to getting back on track is the effect that your success will have on your children. Most children receive mixed messages when they hear their parents say work hard and you can accomplish your dreams or get whatever you want out of life, when mom or dad have not applied this equation towards their personal life. Now your children have a living example at home that this equation:

Hard work + Determination x Motivation = Destination

truly works. Your child can now say "Mom and dad are not just talk. They truly mean what they say. I can see it for myself!"

Your parents and extended family are going to be so proud of you. Whether mom and dad are alive in your life, I know they are smiling and full of pride that their child has a sense of peace about life and is determined to get to the next level, and won't let life hold you back again.

ADVICE FROM OTHERS

Before I close writing this book, I wanted you to read advice from individuals who are dear to my heart and have blessed me with their friendship and words of encouragement. These individuals have all been through adversity at one point in their life and they triumphed over their pain and disappointments to live a life full of purpose. I've highlighted these individuals because I believe that their stories are relatable to all who are reading this book. I've also highlighted them because they are living, true examples of the light at the end of the tunnel. Lastly, I recognize while you are back on track and running your race, you may get tired and weary so let their words inspire you not to get derailed along the way, but to keep trucking. Chooo chooo!!!

ERICKA — SINGLE MOTHER

I have had to overcome a plethora of obstacles throughout my life. All with different effects on my life because some obstacles where smaller personal issues that only hindered me temporarily while others where life changing. I have dealt with lack of time management, family issues, becoming a single mom, being faced with needing to make more money, finding time for a relationship, and what I felt was most important but seemed to have no time for was deciding where I wanted to be in life and how to get there.

There were times when I did not know how I was going to get through but one thing I knew was that I was a child of God and believed that He would see me through. I reached out to people for advice and obtained a mentor. I had to do an inventory and take control of my life. I had to minimize my distractions which included reevaluating the people in my life, their purpose and how they fit into my life. I had to write down my goals both short and long term and look at them daily. At this point, I started to see where I wanted to be and started searching for how I was going to get there.

After great advice from my mentor and best friend, Dr. Sanders, I started putting together a plan. I tackled each fear by writing out how I can overcome that problem. I started saving my money by placing it in an account in which I had no access. I begin to look into the program I wanted to pursue in school and what I needed to do to get there. I walked away from a good paying job where I was unhappy and I am now pursuing my goals. I still have obstacles to face with the adjustment of my life however I have the end goal in sight. I continue to reevaluate my goals and my plan to accomplish them. No matter what I have to do on the back end, I refuse to lose sight of my goal. I no longer have a high paying job, as I am pursuing my educational goals on the contrary. I am happier than I have ever been because I am one step closer to pursuing my dreams.

ROD – SINGLE FATHER

I have discovered different purposes during different season in my life. In High School, my purpose was to fit in. In college, my purpose was to have fun and make money. As a DAD, my LIFE PURPOSE, is to be a father. Being a Father is my passion, and my title. The PF on my business cards stands for Professional Father. This is the focus of my life, at least until my children are grown, and at that point, I may discover another purpose. Purposes can be achieved, and then you need another. Some will take longer, but that is my purpose story!

Success is a Journey. I embraced the journey. While some may think negatively about challenges, difficulties, and failures, I am energized and excited by it. I understand that those are all necessary components of creating substantial success. Therefore, I am excited about gaining experiences that will make me better, and move me closer to my ultimate goal!

I encourage you to minimize your distractions. That is, take control and ownership of what you allow in your psyche. CNN, which stands for Constant Negative News, may be an example. Now I eliminate watching CNN. I also have consciously decided to control my internal thoughts. Are you allowing in too much distraction? Everything is an asset or liability *to what you want to accomplish. Take control and ownership of what you allow in, and value each second!*

Invest in yourself. Attend conferences. I have traveled the world, and invested thousands upon thousands of dollars in personal growth opportunities. Understand that it will cost you much more in the long run, not to get better, than the things you will need to sacrifice today in order to put yourself in a position to gain those growth experiences!

Lastly, a true blessing is only a blessing if you can give it away to someone else. I agree with this. Give back, and do not forget where you came from!

DANYELL – PHD IN BIOCHEMISTRY

Mary J. Blige once said "Never Seek from Man what God has chosen". These words stuck with me as I applied to graduate school in order to obtain my PhD in Biochemistry. These words stuck out because, I was struggling on the GRE (Graduate Record Examination). The GRE is similar to the SAT that I took to get into college. I had a GPA above 3.5, internship experience, was a member of different organizations, and I also had a tight, tear-jerking personal statement. I did not test well; I could not get above a 900 on the GRE and actually, I did not get above that on my SAT. Nonetheless, I still got into college. As a matter of fact, I entered college early through a summer program whose rules were: you take 18 credits over the summer and if you get above a 3.00 GPA then the program would pay tuition, fees, books, and room and broad. And I worked so hard that I not only got above a 3.25, but my colleagues voted me as the most inspirational student. I reflected on this, as I looked at my low score on the GRE while the album, No More Drama played in the background. It was at that moment that I heard Mrs. Mary J. Blige say "Never Seek from Man what God has Chosen".

At that point I knew that my score was not going to determine my future. The next day, I got dolled up, went to class confident and one of my teachers informed me that he spoke with the coordinator at the University of Florida's Chemistry Graduate Program and they wanted to enroll me in their Fall 2003 class. Within 3 weeks of me accepting, I received an email from the coordinator offering me a fellowship that would not only pay for my education, but it also included a laptop!!

In 2006, I obtaining my Masters in Analytical Chemistry, and in 2009 I graduated from UF with my PhD in Biochemistry. I am now studying chemoprevention, issues that affect health disparities, and increasing the knowledge and understanding of science in minority communities. I say all of this to say please do not let test scores hold you back or anything else in life prevent you from achieving your goals You have work hard and sought the face of God, so there is no limit to what you can do!

JAMES — MBA & MARRIED FATHER

I have failed, a lot. However, my failures have driven me. I have learned to think outside of the box because of them. I have learned to listen, but not to let many influence me, because too often, they are thinking based on their limitations. I have to plan based on my own abilities. There's a difference. I know that I am really good at seeing the big picture, and I work at that. I know that failure does not frighten me, and I work at that as well.

My wife left me. She had someone else. When she left, part of what she wanted was for me to chase her. My marriage was a failure. It hurt. Big picture? Even getting her back would not make me happy. She waited for the chase. I filed for divorce quickly and aggressively demanded the time I felt entitled to my son. I am not a weekend daddy. I never had been. Even though people around me were telling me, "She is his mother. There is no way the courts will let you have him half of the time...be happy with the weekends and every other Tuesday," I stuck to my guns. Big picture was I'd had him ALL of the time during the marriage. Half after separation was fair. The judge sided with me. Focusing on the big picture trumped the pain of my failure. I made failure work for me. Others see things and are quick to say, "Never happen." I am that guy that comes back and tells you, "But I did it already."

In addition to having failed, I am stubborn. However, I keep climbing back on that horse after it throws me time and again. I keep getting up when I get knocked down, and there have been times where I was offered some nice incentives to go down and stay down. I figure that if I had to fight through failure and chart trails where there are none, I may as well keep plugging away. I flunked out of undergraduate school twice. I was a sucker for parties. Graduate school was no picnic. Luckily, I had classmates with whom I shared certain traits. I was earning my MBA with a woman who'd had a baby at 14 and a man my age who'd done time for attempted murder. Their lives now are no reflection of their decisions then, but that stubbornness persists. You just aim it to work for you, and you keep pushing until you find what you want. Nobody else's "No" matters. No one believes in me more than me, and I am too hardheaded to forget that.

It has worked for me so far.

PAY IT FORWARD & HELP SOMEONE ELSE

The advice that I and others have shared in this book was to help motivate and inspire you to achieve your dreams. Your personal sense of accomplishment and excitement that you feel from knowing your purpose is great and make us proud! Your hard work and dedication has paid off and guess what, others can see it too! They now want to know how you figured out your purpose in life. They call you for advice about taking classes, they want you to mentor them, and they want you to encourage them as they embark on a similar journey. You are having a major impact on the lives of others around you. Your light is shining ever so brightly that people need blinders on their eyes just to talk to you!!!!

You got the advice, support, and encouragement you needed from this book and I am so very happy for you!! Please pay it forward and help someone else. Pass this book on to them if it has been a benefit for you. Even better, buy them a copy and keep yours as a reference tool later. Everyone deserves to live a purposeful life and I encourage you to be a blessing in the lives of those around you.

What God has destined for you, please don't let no man (and even you) put asunder.

CPSIA information can be obtained
at www.ICGtesting.com
Printed in the USA
LVOW04s1216141116

512885LV00002B/265/P